How to Think Like a Millionaire

[Updated Version]

Dr. Boyce Watkins

DEDICATION

This book is dedicated to every reader who thrives to create and sustain generational wealth.

CONTENTS

PREFACE

I didn't start out to write this book; in fact, this book was born out of a desire to address many of the misconceptions and misnomers surrounding what it requires to become a millionaire. Too often, we make the erroneous assumption that being a millionaire is impossible or highly improbable when the reality is that it is doable and it is a viable option for many of us.

The problem is that many of us do not know where to begin or how to start. This book is comprised of a series of chapters that each addresses ways in which you can position yourself to become a millionaire and it all starts with how you think. It goes without saying that if you shift the way you think, put in the time and the work, and surround yourself with equally committed people then you will be amazed how things will begin to change in your life.

The most important part is that you don't have to do this alone. You can use this book as a blueprint, a reference when you get stuck, and/or as extra motivation and inspiration as you move forward on your quest to become a millionaire.

As always, be educated, stay connected, and continue to strive for excellence!

Dr. Boyce Watkins

CHAPTER 1

THE MILLIONAIRE MINDSET:
THE FIRST FIVE RULES OF ENGAGEMENT

I want you to think back to when you were a child. What were some of the things that you desired? Wished for? How many of those things came to fruition? How many did not? If I were to ask you the difference between the things that became realities and the ones that evaporated, there is probably a strong possibility that your mindset, or attitude towards those things, played a significant role in their actual manifestation.

Believe it or not, the way that we perceive things and think about them can determine if we actually achieve them or acquire them. This is true for wealth, and, more specifically, positioning yourself to become a millionaire. Contrary to popular belief, especially in black communities, being a millionaire is not out of reach and it's not so elusive that only a handful of "special" people have access to it. What if I told you that you, too, can become a millionaire?

Your mindset is instrumental in determining your various levels of personal, professional, and financial success. Specifically, there is something called *The Millionaire Mindset*. There is a way that people think that leads to asset accumulation and there is a way that people think that leads to asset depletion. Now we know that we live in a country that's not fair. We know that we live in a country that has done us wrong. We know that we live in a country that's crooked. We know we live in a country that's corrupt.

However, at the end of the day, when you're dealing with an environment that is competitive, crooked, corrupt, and just downright nasty, there are ways to enhance your chances of survival and there are ways to undermine your chances of survival. There are ways to liberate yourself and there are ways to deepen your enslavement.

When I thought about The Millionaire Mindset, I thought about people I know who have accumulated wealth—not through luck, not through some get rich quick situation, not by getting a record deal, not by signing a NFL contract, not by marriage and not by winning the lotto—I'm talking about people who consistently made decisions on a day-to-day, hour by hour, minute to minute, second by second basis that led to wealth accumulation, as opposed to wealth depletion. That's what I want to share with you in this book.

First, I want to ask you why are you here? I believe that there are a few reasons why you might be here. You might be here because you just want to get ahead and you're tired of getting left behind and for that I commend you because there are a lot of people who are very comfortable being left behind. There are some people who would rather go through the pain of fighting to get ahead and then there are those who would rather allow themselves to fall behind and then simply complain about being left behind.

You also may want to build a better life for yourself and your children and your grandchildren, which you should. Every reasonable and normal man or woman should want a better life for his/her child than he/she had. You don't want your kids to start over from scratch. What kind of craziness is that? Maybe you're tired of being kicked around? I might have to work hard to convince you that you might want money because some people don't want a lot of money or need wealth in order to be happy. Keep in mind that I'm not selling wealth as a key to happiness.

What I'm selling you is freedom. What I'm trying to convince you to buy in to is the idea that you want to be free, so you can make whatever decision you want to make that's going to make you happy. One thing I can say is that when I got freedom, I was much, much happier. I see too many black men who go off the deep end and can't take it anymore and just lose it because they're under so much pressure. Too often, it's related to something financial; frequently, it is related to the fact that they've fallen and they can't get up. They're trying to provide for children that they can't afford to take care of. They don't have the money they need to take care of their family. They have friends with problems and they can't help them. They have problems of their own that they can't solve and those problems often link back to money.

I see a lot of moms going through the same thing. Our communities are filled with single-parent households and there's no person in America that has a lower net worth than the single black mother in America, not one. Maybe you're tired of being kicked around? I can just tell you that freedom is a solution for everybody because even animals understand the value of freedom. You don't have to talk a dog into the value of being free. He knows that instinctively. He doesn't like being in captivity, even if it's comfortable captivity, he still doesn't like that.

You also may want to control your own destiny. A lot of us talk about being products of our environment. I think that is false. If you have enough energy and you're committed to your freedom, then I believe your environment can be a product of you. I believe you can shape your environment. Every parent can shape that household. Those little kids are going to follow you and do whatever you say. They're going to react to whatever you tell them that matters. If you tell them that knowing wealth is more important than understanding Nicki Minaj's lyrics, then they're going to listen to that; they're going to believe that; and they're going to repeat that to their friends.

You probably want the ability to control your own destiny and you do have that power. Also, you can use the power of money to do something positive in your life and the lives of others. It took me a long time to finish school though because I made long-term investments to ensure that when I did finish school, I was going to make a certain amount of money. I made sacrifices some of my friends, actually, a lot of my friends, didn't make in college because many of them went right to work after college. I was in school another seven years because I wanted to position myself so that I could have a chance to make some money.

I deeply resent the idea that when people come up to me and say, "Well, you were just lucky. You're fortunate." I wasn't fortunate. Fortunate didn't make me stay in school another seven or eight years while you were out partying and doing whatever you were doing. I'm sorry, but fortunate didn't push me to keep going for all those years and get a Ph.D. in finance. That was really hard to do, so why give fortunate credit? There's no fortunate involved in that. It required 10 hours a day of studying for seven to eight straight years. That's what that fortunate was.

A lot of times we like to buy in to this idea that those who have resources just got lucky and those who don't have resources are always unlucky. I do believe luck is real; however, there are some people that do get a little bit of luck, but you can't live off of luck. Luck is not sustainable—neither bad luck nor good luck. Ultimately, what I have found is that accumulating wealth gives you the ability to be a better parent; it gives you the ability to be a better friend; it gives you the ability to be a better person if that's what you want to be. Specifically, in the black community, there are a whole lot of people who have financial problems. If you're the person who can help people by investing in them or supporting them when they need you the most, then that allows you to feel better about life in general.

I like the fact that I have a lot of relatives and friends who can say, "Boyce did this for me when I was really down and out. Boyce was able to help me with that." It feels good to be a dad, especially since I have daughters; it feels good to be able to say, "You know what? I want to pamper my daughter a little bit. I'm going to take good care of her." Wealth is something that can enhance your life in a lot of ways.

I'm not trying to sell you on the idea of worshiping money though, so don't ever think that that's the case. I don't think money is a destination. Money is a channel. Money is a tool to reach more important destinations which are freedom and happiness. Money gets you the freedom and freedom gets you the happiness. That's the way it should go. If you don't have happiness and you have a lot of money, then you lost the game. You didn't play the game right.

And it all starts with how you think.

Here's why The Millionaire Mindset is critical to your success. Some of us just don't know how to think. What a lot of people don't know is that there are just rules to the wealth game. There are rules to the way things work. It's not a roll of the dice. I saw someone today who said that when I last suggested investing in the stock market he said, "Well, you might as well go to Las Vegas and play the casino," and I said to myself, "Wow, that's very sad that he thinks investing in the stock market is the same as going to the casino because it's not." My dissertation, my Ph.D. doctoral dissertation, was written on the stock market, so I know that it's not the same as a casino. You can make it into a casino if you want, but they're not the same thing.

There's a lot of misinformation out here about how wealth is accumulated. Why is that? Because it's been made very easy for you to believe that it's all about luck or all about corruption. We tend to think that either someone got lucky or they just stole it all and I know a lot of wealthy people who didn't steal anything.

Also, this concept is based on scientific research, as well as real-world experience. What I lay out and explore in this book is based off of what I have observed and experienced in the real world where I have been around a lot of people who have achieved The Millionaire Mindset. I noticed that there are patterns to their success and common traits and practices that many millionaires share.

Rule number one: Income means nothing until it does. Now I want you to think about that for a second as I move on. I want you to stop focusing on how much money you make. Who cares how much money you make? A lot of people talk about wealth and equality and wealth progress as, "Well, so-and-so makes $1 million a year. So-and-so makes $200,000 a year." The income is not the most important factor.

Actually, it's not just about how much money you make. It's about how much money you keep. You can think of wealth like a water faucet. Water comes out of the faucet. You have income, which represents the water that's coming out, and if you let all the water go down the drain, then guess what? If somebody turns the faucet off, you have no more water to drink. But if you have a bucket that is capturing all the water, even if a little bit of the water is leaking out, at least you will have water in case the faucet turns off.

Metaphorically, the white man's money is the faucet. The water's coming out. Most of us have a big open pit where all that water is coming through the drain and we're taking little sips of it and saying, "Look at me. I'm doing good. I'm drinking good," but then you're not putting a bucket underneath the faucet to capture the water so; therefore, you have no wealth. The water in the bucket is your wealth. The water coming from the faucet is your income.

When you focus on how much money you keep that means you're focusing on what you own, so income should be funneled into ownership. You take the income. You buy things with it that will accumulate and grow in value. You don't buy things that are going to deplete in value. You don't waste all your money and give it all away. You engage in what is called "capital accumulation," which means that you say, "Okay, I have spent 10 years making $50,000 a year. That means I have made $500,000 over that time. I have accumulated about $50,000 in assets and because I have invested these assets, they've grown in value to $150,000 to $200,000." Or "I have taken 10% of that $500,000 I have made and I've spent that $50,000, started a business that now generates $50,000 a year, which in itself becomes a very valuable asset."

Those are the steps to becoming a millionaire when you own assets that generate income when you're not getting income from somebody else. You own your own faucet. The best way to fill up a bucket is to not just have the bucket there when the faucet's on, but your ultimate goal is maybe to somehow get your own faucet, right? Once you have your own faucet and your own bucket, then you're doing good. But if somebody else owns that faucet and you don't have a bucket, then you're going to be broke. As soon as they turn the faucet off, you're dying of thirst.

Rule number two: Cash doesn't matter as much. Income doesn't matter as much. I bring that up because I have seen rappers, especially, show a bunch of cash to try to prove that they're doing well. For example, at one point, the rapper 50 Cent said that he was broke. He was in bankruptcy court. To impress people who don't understand wealth, 50 Cent basically took a bunch of money, $100 bills, and he spelled the word broke out on the floor with the bills.

I saw a lot of people say, "Oh, see I told you, I told you he's not broke. I told you he was doing good." No, that doesn't mean he's doing good. That just means he has cash. Cash and wealth are not usually one and the same. That could be somebody else's cash. If you have a credit card, anybody can get cash. Just take the credit card, borrow a bunch of money off of it and turn it into cash. Then you look like you're rich, but you're not.

There are fake people out here, a lot of fake millionaires out here. Fake millionaires are people who pretend that they have more money than they actually have. Many of these people, unfortunately, are icons in the black community. I know a lot of famous people. I meet people in Hollywood and everywhere else. It would be interesting if I were able to tell you how many of these people really aren't doing nearly as well as they appear to be doing, but all of them have to pretend to be doing well because that's what you glorify. That's what you end up worshiping.

Rule number three: Live by your goals, your desires, and execute your plans. You have to figure out what you want. You have to set a goal to get it and then you have to execute it. Execution is the most important thing in the world. Everybody should have a goal. If you don't have goals in life, then you have no purpose. If you have no purpose, then you're not likely to feel inspired by your life. If you're not inspired by your life, then you're likely to be depressed by your life. Too often, people who are depressed are people who simply are not living in their purpose. Find a purpose, set a goal, and if you want to really be challenged, set an impossible goal.

Most goals never come to life. The reason most goals never come to life is because people don't execute them. They don't follow through. They talk, talk, talk and they think that talking is the same as doing. Many times when I hear business proposals from people about how they're going to become millionaires by building this big business, they do a lot of yip, yip, yapping; yet, they don't put any money into their idea and then that idea just disappears because you didn't bring it to life.

The ability to execute is everything. That's what's going to separate you from all the other millions of people who say they want to be successful and they want to be rich. Pay attention to how many times you ask somebody: "What are you going to do when you grow up?" Young people often respond, "I want to be rich." Then you say, "Well how are you going to get rich?" A lot of them won't have an answer. They won't know.

That's like if I ask you, "Where are you trying to get to?" You say, "Oh, I want to get to California." I say, "Well, how are you going to get there?" and you don't even know where California is. You don't have money for a bus ticket or a plane ticket. You don't know anything. You haven't looked at a map. You don't know what it takes. You don't even know how far away it is. Ultimately, people like that are probably not going to reach their goals because they're not breathing life into their objectives by actually following through.

Potential means nothing if it's not realized. I would take a mediocre idea that's executed over an amazing idea that's not executed. If you come to me and you say, "Boyce, I have a business idea. Is this a good idea?" I might tell you, "Sure, that sounds like a great idea," but you know what? It doesn't matter. What matters is can you answer the key question. The key question is: Are you going to execute your plan? Are you going to invest 10,000, 20,000, 30,000 hours of work over the next 10, 15 years to make it successful? Are you pulling money out of your pocket that you could be spending at Applebee's and actually investing that into your business to make it move forward? If the answer is *yes*, then even a mediocre idea has a chance of becoming successful.

Rule number four: Money must play some role in your day-to-day conversations. We don't talk about money enough and that's why we don't tend to have very much money. People who talk about money a lot usually have money. Those who have money usually talk about money. Just like anything else, people who talk about church a lot tend to go to church. They go to church on a regular basis. They have bibles and stuff around their homes. People who talk about singing and music a lot tend to have great musicians that come out of the family. People that talk about thugging and being a gangster, a Crip or a Blood, tend to have violence in their families. Whatever it is that you speak on is usually going to manifest itself in your life.

A mother who talks about her children a lot is usually going to have a close relationship with her children. She's going to know a lot about where her kids are and be able to tell you a lot about her kids. Those who talk a lot about money, not in a materialistic way but in an empowering way, tend to be the people who know how to have it. Families must talk about money. Get with your family and have conversations about money. It's not taboo. It's not bad. Why would you think it's taboo to talk about something that is essential to your day-to-day existence? Why does it make sense to sit around and not talk about money and then spend all your time worrying about money and going to church and having to pray for money because you didn't plan on how you were going to get any money?

People who tend to have money are people who plan to obtain it. You have to learn to obtain it. You teach your kids how to obtain it. Your kids are going to need money one day. Why would you send them into the world without them knowing how to get the thing that they're going to need every day in order to be free and happy?

I have seen brothers and sisters, young people and older people, just broken down and struggling because they didn't have enough money. Why would you put them out in a world that's built on money without any understanding of how money works? That's like sending them to Donald Trump's house to beg for food because you chose not to feed them. That's not going to work out well for them.

Rule number five: Stop giving your money away. That's very basic, but it's absolutely true. Millionaires are very good about not giving their money away. A lot of millionaires come out of the Midwest. The Midwest is a great place because in the Midwest they don't care about being flashy. They don't care about balling out of control. They don't care a whole lot about driving the nicest cars, living in the biggest houses, or spending $200,000 going to a fancy university, so they avoid student loan debt. They make very good decisions when it comes to not giving their money away.

You don't want to drive your wealth. You don't show how well you're doing by driving the fanciest car on the lot. You do that after you have taken care of everything else. You shouldn't wear your wealth on your head or chest. It doesn't mean that you don't go to the hairdresser, but if getting your hair done becomes the most expensive line item in your budget there's a good chance you may want to reconsider your priorities. Not because getting your hair done isn't important, you should get your hair done. If you want to look good, go look good. The same is true for prioritizing designer clothes.

Ask yourself, "What else in your budget do you have that is as important to you as getting your hair done? What is it in your budget that relates to long-term economic building and power? What line item in your budget is a long-term benefit?" Think about it: Your hair's going to be messed up in about two weeks and that designer will be out of style in two years.

You have to do a self-assessment to determine if those resources should go elsewhere like paying for your child's tutor, so your child can have a good education, which therefore increases his/her chances to earn income. Is it paying to get your child into some sort of program where they can become an entrepreneur? Is it putting aside money so you can buy your first home so that you're not buying a house for your landlord?

What is it in your budget that is as important as getting your hair done? Or to those who love fancy sneakers and you really may want to collect those shoes and think that they're great, but what is it in your budget that is as important as getting those shoes? If you can't figure that out, if you don't have something that's long-term that is as important as the short-term stuff, then that's a real problem, right? You don't want to wear your wealth on your head, chest, or feet.

Most millionaires are very good at asset accumulation because they minimize the number of financial faucets that leak out money from their buckets. Maybe I didn't say that as articulately as I wanted to, but basically, people who have wealth, people who become millionaires are just basically people who have incomes that probably aren't much higher than yours, but they keep what they have and also, they find ways to get more of what they want. That's it. They find multiple streams of income. They widen the streams of income that they already have and then, when they get the money, they keep it. They're not thinking, "Oh, I can't wait to get my tax refund so I can go to the mall," or "I can't wait until I get my paycheck because I want to get those shoes," or "I just sold some stocks so I can go buy me a new car." They don't do that. They're thinking about investing all the time. They're always thinking like investors, not consumers.

Financial faucets may cause leakage in your wealth building strategy. It might be student loan debts. Student loan debt is killing the capacity of families to build wealth all over the country. Car notes are just not a good move. You don't want a big car note. You want a small car note if any car note at all. Credit card companies love it when you borrow money and you have good credit because they know they're going to get their money back and they know they're going to make a profit, so they will get to a point where they will beg you to take money from them because they want you to pay for access to that money.

Corporations absolutely, positively, master the art of psychological manipulation to convince you to go out and buy things that you don't really need. That's what they do. They make you feel like you need to look a certain way and that you need to have a certain lifestyle and they do that to black people the most.

You ever notice how black commercials for cars and stuff, the ones they show on BET, always have a very different feel? They're always very stylish, very sleek, very cool and that's because they've studied the psychology of black people and they know that black people care more about being cool than they care about actually being in good financial health. That's why the commercials are so compelling.

They don't do that with white people. Don't get me wrong, we know white people have their own issues. They have their own form of financial ignorance. We're not letting them off the hook at all. I can show you data that will prove to you that white people are not as financially intelligent as we might think, but I'm talking about black people right now. When you watch these commercials, pay close attention and note how our commercials have a different feel than other commercials and they're not appealing to our logic. They're appealing to our emotions and your desire to be cool, flashy and hip because they know that's what matters to many of us.

Rule number six: Move in silence. If you're trying to accumulate wealth, one way to stop the financial leakage is to stop inviting people into your space that are going to drain you of what you have. Entertainment teaches people to brag about their wealth. Every time you watch a video, rappers are always throwing money up and doing stuff like that because their low self-esteem pushes them to want others to look up to them in a certain way because of their so-called success.

You will hear rappers, like Future, in a recent song say, "Look at the car I have. Look at the money I have. I am a model of success, even though I am making music that is killing my community. It's okay because look at how much money I have. Look at how successful I am look at how flashy I am." I would be willing to bet you that if you were to look at Future's bank account, while he might have some investments, I'm not saying that he doesn't, I would be willing to bet you that his expenses are insanely high. I bet you a lot of the expenses are on things that aren't going to have much, if any value whatsoever, in 10 years.

Again, I'm not talking about him in particular, I'm talking about all of us and the fact that we tend to emulate what we see immediately. I will tell you, people that I know who really have liquid wealth don't tell a lot of people how much money they have. It's a very bad idea to brag about how much money you have. Bragging tends to make you a target. It draws attention from people that might want to steal from you. A lot of rappers get robbed because they tell everybody how much they have and then they show up in town and the killers are waiting with the guns. It's like, "Okay, this guy has money, so we're going to go get him." Also, you have relatives who will guilt trip you into the ground to borrow money from you. You have to have a policy on how you deal with relatives who want money. My policies are pretty basic. In fact, I could do a whole book on how I deal with relatives and money. I follow the C-O-S-T model of cooperative economics, which we teach in the Black Wealth Boot Camp. I formulated that model for cooperative economics: contribute, own, save, invest and target.

Basically, I tell people, and I repeat it all the time, that trade is better than charity. That means that if you come to me and you want charity, I might give you an ounce of charity, but I'll give you a pound of trade, meaning that if you ask me for $100 for charity just because you're having a hard time, I'm going to come back to you with a counter proposal.

If I see that you're sitting around and you don't have a job and you have free time, I'll say, "How about this? I'll give you $500, but you have to come work for me for a week or two weeks or whatever it is." Or "I know that you're good with computers, so I'll give you five times more than you ask for, but you have to give me something too. You have to give something to the family business in order to earn this money." I do this with my kids. I do this with everybody.

Also, if you ask me for an amount of money I'm not comfortable giving you, I'm not going to always say no if I love you because I don't think that's right. I don't think it's right to just neglect family members, but what I'll do is I'll pick an amount that I'm comfortable with and I'll say, "Here's my contribution. Now you can't say I didn't do anything for you."

Ultimately, you have to have a policy for dealing with that because when you're the best person in your group or you're doing better than all of the people around you, chances are you're going to be the one they're going to look at when it's time to pay the check when you go out to dinner. You're the one they're going to come to when they have financial problems. You have to learn about people and human behavior just as much as you learn about money.

In fact, I don't really tell people how much money I have. Because I am a public figure, they assume whatever they're going to assume. I will let them assume things, but you won't see me going around bragging about any of that, unless it's maybe for educational purposes so I can prove to those who don't think I know what I'm talking about that I do know a little bit about what I'm talking about.

CHAPTER 2

THE MILLIONAIRE MINDSET: THE FINAL FIVE RULES OF ENGAGEMENT

In chapter one, I explored the first five rules of engagement. These rules, like the ones in this chapter, are intended to be guiding points that can help you measure how effectively you are engaging in behaviors and making decisions that are aligned to *The Millionaire Mindset.* As you go through these, take the time to pause and process the information. Most importantly, think about its applicability to your life.

Rule number six: Learn financial fertility. Learn the concept of financial fertility. That's another concept, another theory I put together just for black people. You won't read this in a textbook anywhere that I know of. I didn't learn it in school. I created this concept for black people to help you understand wealth and how it works.

For most Americans, your money dies either a fast death or a slow death. A fast death is when you spend it and you give it all away. A slow death is when you don't invest your money and your money does not grow. Inflation erodes the value of your dollar consistently over time. It eats away at it. The same way Pablo Escobar, the big drug dealer, used to lose $2 billion a year because the rats ate the money. That's what inflation is. It's a rat that eats away at your money if your money is not working.

Your money is a living thing. It is a living, growing creature. That dollar bill has the capacity to give birth to other dollar bills if you don't cut out it's womb from the time you get it, meaning that if you kill the fertility, then it's not going to grow. It's not going to grow into anything. But if you allow it to be fertile, you plant it in fertile soil. Then you can live off of that money for the rest of your life and then your grandchildren can live off of that money for the rest of your life. This is financial fertility.

I heard a story just yesterday from a friend. Someone's grandparents bought a house 70 years ago. The whole family lived in this house and the children lived there and then when the children became adults, they stayed in this house. It was a big house. It had little old apartments in it, so the children were all able to live in this house rent free and then the grandchildren were able to live in this house rent free. When the grandparents died, they sold the house to the child for a dollar. Now the child owns the house and other relatives are allowed to live in this house for nothing.

I said that's a beautiful thing that they owned this and generationally, others are guaranteed to have a place to live. That's a model that most people don't understand. Most people cannot envision saving by sacrificing. They don't even know what that would look like.

Ultimately, when you talk about financial fertility, it's about understanding that money is not meant to be spent. Money is a seed. Seeds are supposed to be planted, not eaten. When you spend money, they call it consumption because you're eating your financial seeds. When you spend your money, you're killing the fertility of that money. That dollar will never do anything for you. It leaves your community. It leaves your family. It leaves your pocket forever. But when you plant that seed, it can grow forever.

I want you to think of the example of what I call "the money rabbits." This is another analogy I came up with to help you understand what I'm talking about here. Let's say that you love bunnies and you want to have as many bunny rabbits as you can. You could do it the hard way by just going to a store to buy them. Let's say that bunnies are $10 each and you can save $50 to buy five. You then save $50 more to purchase another five. You continue to purchase them in $50 increments. That's the hard way to do it.

Because if you're smart what you would do is understand the fertility of bunny rabbits and you would get five males and five females. You would put them in a pen. You would turn down the lights, turn on some Marvin Gaye and let nature take its course. After two or three generations, you would have bunny rabbits all over the place.

Here's the beautiful thing. When you get to later generations, every time you move forward, you will have more rabbits in each generation. Maybe in the first fertility cycle, the 10 rabbits produce 20. But then during the second cycle, the 20 rabbits might produce 60. In the third cycle, the 60 rabbits might produce 150. It becomes a snowball effect where you don't have to do anything else. You don't have to spend any more money because you planted the seed.

Money is the same way. Compound interest is the same way. Albert Einstein said that compound interest is the eighth wonder of the world. He said it's the greatest force in the universe because he couldn't understand how money grows that fast. That's what they call growing exponentially. Growing linearly, is when it's just straight up. You're just working hard and doing it in a straightforward fashion. Exponential is non-linear because it resembles a curve; it accelerates at an increasing rate. It means the more you get, the more you're going to get and that's the way money is.

That's why you have people in this economy where it seems like they are just made of money. Money just falls in every direction. They can't stop making money. Why is it that you have some people who feel that they can't get a break? They can't get ahead? They can't get any money? Then you have people who can't stop making money. Money is just everywhere. Well, that's because of the fertility concept. It's about where you are.

When people say that it takes money to make money, you don't always have to have money to make money, but having money does help you make money. But you have to get the ball started. If you don't get the ball started, then it's never going to get anywhere. Think about this. You will never chop down an apple tree to get firewood, right? Because if you chop down your apple tree to get firewood, you will never get apples again. Instead the smart person says, "I have an apple tree. It can feed me now. It can feed me later. It can feed me for the next X number of years. I'm going to keep my apple tree."

Rule number seven: I want you to learn what it means to be a millionaire. A lot of people don't know what it means to be a millionaire. Being a millionaire doesn't mean you have $1 million in cash. It doesn't mean that you make $1 million a year. It means that you have $1 million in net worth. That means if you take the value of all your assets, subtract the value of your liabilities, all your debt and everything else, that net worth is over $1 million.

When I knew I was a millionaire was when I looked at my businesses and I used a formula to determine the value of my businesses. I did the calculations and I said, "Okay, I think we have reached 1 million in status." Ultimately, even my name: Dr. Boyce Watkins, is worth millions of dollars because I invested in my brand. That is an asset I can pass down to my children. 50 years from now, if they run the business right, my children will be able to put my name on a product and it will be able to make money for them. My grandchildren, and my great grandchildren who aren't even born yet will be able to benefit from the assets that we have accumulated in this generation.

Your children and grandchildren and great-grandchildren will also be able to benefit from assets that you have accumulated, including a home that you buy. (Think about my example of the person who bought a house 70 years ago and the family is still living in it in 2017). Maybe it will be from stocks that you own. If you bought $40 or $50 worth of Coca-Cola stock in 1919 or 1920, then that would be worth millions of dollars right now. Nike stock,

Amazon stock, and all of the stocks that you're buying right now will generate wealth if you hold on to it. Those assets that you accumulate will allow people beyond your generation to benefit.

When people say, "Well, when do we sell? When should I sell my stock? When should I sell my house?" I say, "Well, if you don't have to sell, then why would you sell? Why? Why are you thinking that this wealth game is something that's supposed to end when you die? Don't you know anything about the afterlife?"

One thing I do know about the day I die is that the world will keep spinning and my children will keep being black. They're still going to deal with racism. There are going to be grandchildren and great grandchildren who are going to need money just like I did. That's what I know about the afterlife, so when I tell you I'm preparing for the afterlife, I'm not preparing for my afterlife. I don't know exactly where I'm going to be. Maybe, I'll be in heaven. Maybe I'll be somewhere else. I'm not talking about that. I'm talking about the more important afterlife, which is not what happens to me, but what's going to happen to them.

When you accumulate an asset, stop thinking that there's an end game and a point where you sell it and you just take your money and you go to the club and throw it up in the air and go to Las Vegas and just live it up. No, there's not supposed to be an end game. You're part of a relay race. You're going to hand the baton off and you have to run as fast as you can so that your kids are going to be able to be further in the race than you were.

Most millionaires don't have $1 million in the bank. That's one thing I want you to understand about being a millionaire. Also, most wealthy families that are worth $10 million, $20 million, $100 million, whatever, most of those families had a generation that began the accumulation process and passed the baton properly. They continued the accumulation process and by the third generation, the family is worth $200 million or $300 million.

Every person reading this right now, every black person reading and every non-black person too, please note that in two generations, you can have a family wealth that's valued at over

$100 million if you take very basic steps now. Any person in poverty 100 years ago who had a consistent investment strategy, who had a Millionaire Mindset, could easily have a family today that's worth millions and millions of dollars and I'm not making that up. That's theoretically true.

Also, most millionaires are what they call illiquid in their early stages. Chances are if your journey is anything like mine, you will be what some might call a paper millionaire. Where you can look at your assets minus your liabilities and say, "Okay, I'm a millionaire now on paper, but I don't feel like a millionaire." I didn't feel like a millionaire. I didn't have money just flying out of my ears and money to burn when I first hit that million in status.

It was very hard. I was like, "God, I have worked my butt off and I've built all this, but I don't feel like I am really doing as well as I thought I would be," and so you're going to have that stage maybe where you're illiquid. It all depends on how you get there.

Being illiquid and not having cash does not preclude your ability to be a millionaire and having cash doesn't really say much about your financial situation at all, honestly, other than the facts that you have access to cash. It's almost like somebody saying that, "Well, I saw Joe in a car. Therefore, he must own a car." Anybody who understands how cars can be acquired knows that that's not true. Joe could have borrowed that car from his friend. Joe could have gotten a car note from a car dealer. There are a lot of ways Joe could have gotten that car besides owning the car free and clear. Don't think just because somebody is holding something that that's what they actually own.

Rule number 8: Learn every mode of economic transportation. What does that mean? Now imagine if you're driving to California, then you want to go Hawaii so that's your goal. You're in New York. You want to get to California, then you want to go to Hawaii. Well, what if somebody told you that the best way to get to California was, "Oh, you just start walking really fast." You say, "Well wait. California is a long walk I don't want to walk there." He says, "No, just walk fast. If you walk fast you will get there a little faster than you would if you walk slow. It's better than crawling. It's better than sitting still."

Well, yeah that might be true and you can still get to California by walking, but my God, there are other ways to do that. Well, that's what happens when people tell you that the best way to have a lot of money is to go work for somebody. Then if you say, "I want to have more money," they tell you "Well, you just have to work harder to work more hours and get a second job or get a higher paying job." That's like somebody saying, "Well, if you want to get to California, just walk really fast."

What's happened is they've limited you because they haven't told you about all the other ways that you can go to California. We do that to our children every single day. We tell our kids, "Boy, you want some money? You best go get a job." Okay, that's Plan D maybe or that's one of the options. What about all the other options?

I bet you that when Donald Trump talks to his little boy, Barron, he reminds him that one day, he will take over the family empire. That's why he gave him the name Barron. Barron's royalty. It's like when we name our children King and Leader and things like that. Then, too, I bet you that when they talk about making money, I bet you they've never, ever talked about Barron getting a job, unless it was to work for his father so that he could learn how to eventually run the family business.

But the interesting thing is that we talk about getting jobs all the time. We cheer for each other when we get jobs. We cheer harder when somebody gets a job than when they make an investment. We cheer harder when you got a promotion than we do when you escape the plantation and start your own company. Why would you do that?

That's very interesting. That's like someone cheering harder for you because you got to be a babysitter than if you actually had a baby. You see if you're a babysitter, you might love that child, but that isn't your baby.

When you go to work every day, you are an economic babysitter, you're babysitting somebody else's economic enterprise. But when you have your own child, that child might be little and it might be fragile; it might even be a preemie baby sitting up in the little heat lamp barely holding on, but that's *your baby*. That's where your attention needs to be, not on babysitting somebody else's child. Don't let your little baby die because you're off babysitting someone else's child. That doesn't make any sense, but that's where the psychosis can come into play. That's where we get it backwards.

Remember, there are some other modes of transportation. If you're trying to go to California, sure you could drive. You could also ride a bike if you want. You could take a bus. You could ride a plane or helicopter. If you're trying to get to Hawaii, which is like getting to the upper echelons of wealth, there are some places economically that you simply cannot get to by having a job, even if it's a good job.

If you get Lebron James' job, there's only one of those jobs, maybe Steph Curry gets the other one. If you get Lebron James' job, you can certainly do really well for yourself and go very, very far. But by getting Lebron James' job, you will never get as far as the person who signs Lebron James' check. You will not get as far as Dan Gilbert who owns the Cleveland Cavaliers.

Lebron, himself, will at some point have to develop an economic helicopter, where he is investing in multiple businesses on a large scale that allow him to really make the kind of money that will put him in the billionaire status. Michael Jordan made that transformation. He's not making basketball player money anymore and he made a lot of money as a basketball player. He is now making the money of a business owner, of an investor.

At the end of the day, you just have to know all of the different methods of economic transportation that go outside of just walking to work every day. This leads me to the next rule.

Rule number nine: Make sure you know the game that you're playing. Well, here's the thing: Capitalism, in itself, runs America. Simply put, America is a capitalist society. It isn't going to stop being capitalist no matter how hard you pray that it's going to change. It's not going to stop being racist. It's not going to stop being greedy. It's not going to stop not caring about the poor.

There will never be a point in America in your lifetime where America will truly show that it really cares about providing economic opportunities to everyone. It won't do that.

America is a country that's built on the survival of the fittest. If you have the information and you know how the game works, then you're going to get ahead. If you didn't get the information, either because somebody didn't tell you or you just chose not to pursue it or you spent your time on your cell phone looking up comedy videos instead of education, then guess what? You will just get thrown in the economic dumpster like everybody else.

Basically, capitalism is a horse and jockey game. Let me explain. Imagine a horse race and the jockey is riding the horse. The jockey doesn't really do any work, right? He doesn't run an inch, but he controls the horse. He's telling the horse what to do and he can manage and manipulate the horse. He can pick the right horse to ride and then when they cross the line together, the jockey gets all the rewards.

The horse gets a little hay. When he gets too old, they shoot him or if he breaks his leg, they shoot him because he's no longer of use to the system, but the jockey gets all the money, gets all the fame, and gets the wreath of roses around his neck. The jockey gets the benefits of the horse's hard work.

Well, in this economy, there are people who train themselves to be jockeys and people who train themselves to be horses. It starts a lot with what your parents taught you when you were a kid. It starts a lot with your value system. Basically, the economic jockeys in America are the people who own the stock, the stock investors, and the jockeys are people who own real estate and also the people who own small and large businesses because business owners are the other jockeys.

For the people who own stocks, their horses are consumers. People who will get their refund check and run straight to the mall; you probably know a whole bunch of people like that. They walk around with the Gucci bags and whatever because they're feeling good about themselves because they gave away all their money and now they're looking fly. So, you bought your flyness and got nothing of economic value in exchange because whatever you think is fly in 2017 won't be so cool in the year 2027, so it's not as if you have anything that has any long-term value.

The horses for the people who own property are the renters. When you rent property over a long period of time, it is the most amazing economic mind-trick known to man. You spend years and years paying money to buy property that is going to belong to somebody else. When you are done paying rent over a 20-year period, someone else is going to own that house and give it to their kids and your kids are going to start over with nothing.

It is amazing that people can actually play that game and people fall for it. It's astonishing. Yeah, it's hard to become a property owner. There is some work that's involved, but I see a lot of black folks accomplishing other things that require a lot more work that aren't nearly as important. I think it's actually harder to learn the lyrics to all the songs on the radio than it is to figure out how to buy a house. I think it's harder to learn all the little line dances that come out than to invest in my 401(k) or learn how to buy property and run a business.

I don't know anything about the storyline of *Scandal*, *Love and Hip Hop* or any of the other garbage that's being fed to people by the media, but I do know the basics of financial literacy and I do know what my stock portfolio did this week. A lot of times, our priorities are really what play a big role in terms of what we know.

The horses for the people who own businesses are the employees. It doesn't mean that you can't be an employee or a renter or a consumer at some point. A lot of people consume things. I consume things every day pretty much. I have rented things. I have rented facilities to do venues. I have rented apartments. A lot of us rent things and a lot of us have worked for other people. There's nothing wrong with that. There's nothing wrong with any of that.

The problem with that is when you do it *all of the time*. When all you are is a renter, a consumer, and an employee and you never think about being an owner of a business, an owner of property or an investor, whether it's in the stock market or anything else, then effectively you're like the perpetual horse. It's like the difference between the person who eats sugar when they just want to have something sweet versus a person who has a whole diet that's nothing but sugar and cake and ice cream and they don't ever eat anything healthy.

That's what happens when you are a person who only consumes and only rents and only works for other people. In other words, take the time to check where you are in the game. Are you the horse or are you the jockey? Maybe sometimes you have to be the horse, but do you, at least, get to be the jockey sometimes? Remember, all of the rhetoric about being a billionaire and wealth building is really a game with rules that can be understood by everyone.

Imagine that you're playing in a Super Bowl but you don't know the game? You wake up one day and somebody has dropped you in the middle of the Super Bowl and the Patriots are on one side and the Falcons are on the other. They're running at you at 100 miles an hour. You have no training and you're not in shape so you don't know how to run. You don't have any strength. Whereas, the other players have been training the whole year.

You have never seen a football, so you don't even know exactly what's happening around you. You don't know where the goal line is, so even if you had the ball, you wouldn't know which way to run for it. In fact, you wouldn't know which goal line to run to. *You don't know the rules to the game.*

If you're in that game and you don't know the difference between the cheerleaders and the referees and the quarterback versus the running back, then what will effectively happen is you would be killed. You would be slaughtered in the middle of that game because nobody prepared you for that game. That's what happens when you take an 18-year-old black child and you drop him/her in to the economic system, into a competitive economic system and they have no training whatsoever. They're not prepared for any of it.

That young black boy, who has never been taught to create

his own job and who's never been taught to save money, to invest, or to do anything, is going to be killed. He is going to die either a fast death or a slow death. He is going to end up where a lot of these other young black men end up, becoming suicidal or aborted from a society where they don't even matter anymore.

If we go back to the football analogy, it's like some of us are dropped in the middle of that football field and we're trying to survive in a competitive game that is unfamiliar. You are probably going to end up having to become a slave to somebody else because the only thing you can do is huddle up behind someone who can protect you.

For men that's incredibly emasculating. We end up hoping that somebody else protects us and in exchange for protection, there is slavery. That's how the world works. In turn, this can lead to victimization. Those who play the game on your behalf, who teach you the rules, might say, "Oh, well here's how it works. When you get the ball, you're supposed to hand it to me and I'm supposed to go run in the end zone and score a touchdown."

You say, "Well, wait, I heard, from some radical crazy guy, Dr. Boyce Watkins, that when you run the ball, I'm supposed to tackle you, so that I can defend my goal?" They're going to say, "No, Boyce is a racist. That's wrong. That's crazy and I thought we were friends. Let's partner together. I'll score all the touchdowns and I'll get all the points, but I'll give you a percentage of all the points I earn."

At the end of the game, you don't know why you lost. You end up looking at the scoreboard and you're like, "Wait a minute. You're telling me that this game is fair and you're telling me what the rules are supposed to be. Why does every game end with a score of 186 - 12? Why do I always end up losing in this game?"

It's because you didn't know the rules and you allowed your opponent to teach you the rules, so that's what happens when you send black children to be educated by white people on how the world works. They're not going to teach economic empowerment ever in a white school. They're not going to do it. They're going to teach economic slavery to everybody who is dumb enough to listen.

Everyone who is not prepared will be trained to be a slave and that's it. They will never train you to be free because teaching you freedom requires that somebody loves you and they don't love you.

Rule number ten: Learn what wealth actually looks like. You want to learn what wealth actually looks like. A lot of people don't even know because they are not around people who have accumulated wealth. We tend to think that wealth has to do with cash. We also think wealth has to do with material possessions or how much money your business is making, and that's just not true.

I mentioned this earlier in this chapter, but I'll say it again. Wealth has almost nothing to do with money. Remember, there was a time when there was no money, so how did people know who the rich people were compared to the poor people? Well wealth is about resources, right? Wealth can be your labor. I have never known a healthy unemployed person who wasn't wealthy, ever. The reason I say that is because when you're sitting at home waiting for someone to pay you money for your labor that means that your labor has value. That means that some employer sees value in you.

Unfortunately, we don't see the value in ourselves, especially the value of our time and talents. We often tend to measure our wealth based upon how other people perceive us or even label us. Remember, just because someone else does not see your value does not mean that you don't have value. We have to shift the way that we think about that which is valuable and it starts with us, not an employer, not a corporation, and definitely, not with society.

Instead of using that labor to build something of your own, what we do is devalue it by sitting at home, watching TV all day, or waiting for someone to find us and/or offer us opportunities. In other words, we wait for somebody to acknowledge our value and compensate us. It's like having gold in my backyard and all I do is wait for somebody to come in to buy the gold. Maybe I can actually dig that gold up and sell it myself? Do I really need someone else to tell me that it is valuable and worth money? Of course not. Well, the same is true for you.

Your ability to generate wealth is intricately linked to your abilities, gifts, talents, and resourcefulness. Remember, now that you know how to play the game, you need to know what winning the game looks like.

All relationships have some value. When you have people that come together, they share ideas and relationships and everything. Wealth grows when people come together. London became the first city in the Western Hemisphere to have over a million people in it and one of the richest cities in the world because they had a river that came through London and that's where people gathered.

When you have a gathering of people and they're doing trade, then wealth is developing because of natural resources. Africa was one of the wealthiest continents on earth. That's why everybody wanted a piece of it. To this day, Africa is one of the wealthiest continents on this earth when it comes to all of the natural resources that are there. However, because of colonialism and capitalistic exploitation, many of us perceive that Africa is one of the poorest continents when in fact, it is not.

Just as countries produce natural resources, you are a resource. Think about it: Human Resources is the name of the department that hires for most companies. Why? Because your capital is a resource for that particular company.

Your time, creativity, and ideas are valuable. Ideas have wealth in them in the sense that they have potential. If you execute the ideas, then they can turn into something amazing. If you let ideas just sit there and rot, then they're not going to do anything.

What I do is I keep my ideas. I have idea vaults where I just jot down all the ideas that come to mind because my brain is always moving stuff and generating information. I'm like, "Oh, I'm going to do this. Oh, I really want to do that." But a lot of times I don't have the money and the time to breathe life into those ideas. I might say, "You know what, Boyce? You're not serious yet, so let me put this on a piece of paper and save it so that when you're ready to put money behind the idea and time into the idea, the idea can grow." But ideas are worth a lot if you execute them. If you don't execute them, they don't mean anything.

I hear from a lot of people who have great ideas and great business proposals, yet they haven't done anything with them. Or, maybe they came up with the idea yesterday and they got excited because they felt like it was a great idea, but they haven't actually put any skin in the game. Well then the idea is still dead. Your idea doesn't really mean a whole lot if you haven't given it life. You're like the mother who says, "Well, I just had sex; I got pregnant, and I just had a baby," but you're not feeding the baby. You're letting the baby just sit there. That doesn't make any sense. Just because you conceive something or even give birth to it, that is not the same thing as nurturing, protecting, and investing in it in thoughtful and deliberate ways.

You're probably wealthy right now and you *don't even know it*. If you want to see the wealth in your family, gather the people who you respect and pool them together. Just talk about ideas on how you can build businesses, how you can build wealth, and some other things you could do to make a couple of dollars right now. Don't try to make $1 million, try to make $10. Try this and you will be amazed by how the discussion of ideas, the sharing of information, and just the collective energy of being on one accord can generate things that are actually profitable.

See if you could get together with people and have no money at all and say, "What can we do right this second that can make $10?" And then figure it out and then extrapolate on it and grow on that. Then it's just a matter of time before that idea goes from the concept stage to full implementation. That same group can then begin to ask, "Okay, now we have our $10 idea. What's our $100 idea? After we get our $100 idea, what's our $1000 idea?"

This is not an oversimplified way to think about becoming a millionaire. As with many self-made millionaires, it was an idea that served as the catalyst for a product or service. Wealth did not happen in a vacuum.

When you approach wealth from this perspective, you will have the ability to see all of the wealth that's around you that doesn't involve money and that you are not tapping into. It's very dangerous to fall into the myth that most wealth comes from money. The reason it's very dangerous is because white people have most of the money.

If you think that wealth is *only* about money and you don't have any money and white folks have all the money, then you're naturally going to think that they're better than you, that they're better off than you and that you need them in order to be successful. You don't need money to generate wealth. I have seen it happen a thousand times. What you need is desire and you need some creativity; you need some skill; you need some vision; you need to have a commitment to this idea that you can build something on your own.

Once you have a firm grasp on these 10 rules then you will position yourself to not only become a millionaire, but engage in the behaviors, the mindsets and even the spending habits that most self-made millionaires practice. It's not all about flash and making an impression.

There were people who had great wealth just a decade ago, only to find themselves destitute today. This doesn't mean that these people can never rise again, it simply means that they are not tapping into their true value or ability to generate wealth.

If we can change our mindsets and begin to see how we, too, are and can be millionaires, we can move away from this pervasive idea that Black folks have and always will be poor. If this narrative were true then how is it that cities like Baltimore, Chicago, DC and Detroit have families that can demonstrate generations of wealth, even against the backdrop of Jim Crow and other societal injustices?

We are neither poor in spirit, poor in wealth or poor in opportunities to generate wealth. As you reflect back over Chapters 1 and 2 and the 10 rules that were explored in these chapters, I encourage you to put them into practice in your daily life.

Regardless of what you were raised to believe or what you have been taught about black people and wealth, you do have choices and you do have opportunities to change your life trajectory and that of the people who you love and care about.

CHAPTER 3

FOCUSING ON THE PROCESS OF BECOMING A MILLIONAIRE

Get rich quick is hurting our Black communities. We want everything and we want it now. Somehow, we have been programmed to think that overnight success is the only type of success worth celebrating. Renita was discovered on YouTube and was offered a million-dollar singing contract; Jamal just signed a lucrative deal to play with an NBA team. On the surface, we just see the end result or the prize. What we don't see is the process that was needed in order for them to earn those accolades.

What we don't see are the hours of lessons or practice that they engaged in or the personal sacrifices that were made in order to position them to be successful. This is also true when we talk about the process of becoming a millionaire. Yes, it is a process.

Let me be very clear that it's okay to get rich slowly. In fact, most wealthy people get rich slowly. It is one of the ways that they are able to build and sustain their wealth (which I will discuss in the next chapter). If you study the trajectory of most millionaires and even billionaires who are self-made, you will discover that they did not get rich fast. They did not sign a record deal. They did not get to the NFL. They did not get discovered by somebody in Hollywood. Please get those ideas out of your head and stop feeding them to your children.

Too often, when I go into schools and I ask young people what they aspire to be, they tie their monetary success to someone else's empire. We have to unlearn this and reinforce that it is perfectly ok to generate your *own* wealth from your own ideas. Being dependent, exclusively, on someone else is a laborious process. It's not only a hard way to make money, but it's a false way to make money that too many of us in the black community have bought into without even questioning the logic of it.

Most of the people who I know personally who have made it big in entertainment, often ask, "What is this? This is not what I thought it was going to be." A few of them do okay because they parlay that fame into other things, but a lot of them find themselves disillusioned because they are still hoping for that big "break" that will propel them to stardom, great riches, and fame.

Hollywood, for example, is filled with basically a graveyard of Black African-American brands that were built in the 70s, 80s and 90s. Many of those people don't know what to do with those brands. They might say, "Well, I was really famous because I was on this show that was really popular in 1994 and now everyone in the black community knows me, but I am living in a trailer park because I don't have the ability to do anything with my life because I'm struggling like that."

In this scenario and with many others, a person has handed over his/her destiny to someone else. It's as if we are still waiting for someone to give us permission to shine or to nurture our talents. It's like a grown man standing in front of a refrigerator. He's hungry and there's food in the refrigerator, yet he's waiting for someone else to open the door for him or to give him permission to open the door. Sounds silly, right?

Too often, during the wealth building process, we do the same thing. We have the raw, natural resources that are needed and we have the drive and desire, but we don't fully execute.

For many of us, it is because we don't know how. Well, let me demystify the process for you.

If you don't have the ability to understand how wealth works and how to monetize what you have around you, then you're begging for destitution. What I see a lot of times, using the Hollywood example to go further, is people who have multi-million-dollar brands and what they're doing is they're waiting for a white guy from some big studio to come and monetize that brand for them.

This is a process that I like to call "set it and forget it" when it comes to wealth building. That means that someone will invest small amounts of money every week into maybe the stock market, maybe in their small business, maybe in a property, etc. and they will just wait it out.

You add to that an investment in one's self, specifically and investment in knowledge and you have created a powerful force. For example, if you trust me and you like learning from people like me, you can keep coming back, maybe you can sign up for one of the classes. They don't cost much more than going to the movies, but they will change your life forever.

To me, when you have the combination of consistently investing and you conjoin it with a regular investment of time, knowledge and learning, then you become an informed citizen who has resources to work with.

For those of you who like the sport of basketball, let me offer you the following illustration.

It's like a basketball team where you have a great basketball player like a Lebron James. He has great teammates and he's on his home court. He can do a lot of amazing things when he has something to work with like a master chef who has all the best food available or a master warrior who has all the best weapons available.

That's what happens with your money. Your money is like your weapon and your training as a warrior becomes the skill that you have that allows you to know what to do with those weapons.

Or think about a carpenter who is talented. He gives his best and has learned the latest technology on carpentry; as such, he can be an absolute beast when it comes to building whatever he sees, whatever he wants.

This is power.

That's what happens when you understand how the process of thinking like a millionaire works. You have accumulated some resources to play with and you become the greatest captain of your destiny that you have ever imagined. You are not waiting for a savior, a superhero or a knight in shining armor to save you. You are not waiting for anyone or anything because to understand the process, you embrace it as a part of your journey to becoming a millionaire.

You then gain an inability to sit around and feel sorry for yourself. You see, a lot of us are trained to do that. We're trained to believe that we can't change our condition. We're trained to believe that everybody else gets all the breaks; everybody else gets lucky. Although it may be tempting to embrace this mindset, it is counterintuitive to you becoming a millionaire. It doesn't help you and it definitely does not help you accomplish your stated goals.

Ask yourself: Since when does feeling sorry for yourself ever help you accomplish anything in a competitive society? Since when does feeling bad about being black make you less black? Since when does telling white people about our suffering make them actually do more to help us as a community? Since when can you actually have an empowered community when you're begging for something to carry you?

If you study any period of history, you will clearly see that it doesn't work that way. It's not going to work that way, *ever*.

Most millionaires get there on autopilot. They create systems and infrastructures that allow them to monetize their products and services. They invest in themselves; they master their crafts; and they surround themselves with people who will help to elevate their brands in a sustainable and measurable way. It is not luck and it's definitely not coincidence, or by accident. It is deliberate. There's some sort of consistent strategy of investing over time.

For those of you who still don't see the process, let me offer you an example of accumulation that you have been doing your whole life that you probably haven't thought about. Imagine if you were to add up all of the money you've spent on fast food over the years? Think about that for a second. Think about how frequently you've gone and the amount of money you averaged every trip.

Being honest, most of us have eaten at fast food restaurants more than we care to admit. Let's say that there was a magical "do over button" and you had access to all of the money you have spent on fast food since 1995? Imagine that.

Imagine that between coffee, sandwiches, fries, and shakes, you spent $50 a week. $50 a week is about $2500 a year. I know people spend a lot more than $50 a week on fast food. $2500 a year is $25,000 every 10 years. That's $75,000 over a 30-year period, but that's not the travesty of it. $75,000 is a lot of money, but it's bigger than that—remember, this chapter is all about the importance of process.

Let's circle back to financial fertility from Chapter 1. If you had invested that same amount with the same consistency in the stock market over the same amount of time, that would actually be nearly $1 million dollars. If you had heard this conversation in 1995 and simply said to yourself, "Look, I'm going to keep being who I am. Forget Boyce, he's not going to change my lifestyle. I'm going to keep being me. I like to go to Popeyes Chicken on Thursdays. I'm going to keep doing it."

Obviously, I cannot control what someone does, nor do I want to. But, what I do want to do is help you to see how a different process can lead to different results. You could have said, "I'm going to make sure that I consider my long-term economic strategy and my long-term plan. It has to be as important to me as spending money at Popeyes Chicken. I will make sure that every time I go spend $10 at Popeyes, I put $10 in my stock portfolio. Every time I go spend $8.00 at McDonald's, I put $8.00 into my small business."

If you had done that in 1995 you would be a *millionaire.* Why?

Because most millionaires don't get rich quickly. They get rich very slowly. They get rich over 10, 20, 30-year periods and then their children are the ones who actually get to start the game at the top of the pile and not the bottom. They're the ones who are in that top 1%. They're the ones, unfortunately, who are going to have friends who will say, "Oh, well the only reason that your family has money is because y'all got lucky," when really a lot of those people have the same opportunities you have.

The question is: What are you going to do *now* with those opportunities?

What is your mindset?

90% of wealth building is psychological. The majority of wealth building is totally psychological and if you don't believe that, then I don't know what to say because I have studied financial psychology. In fact, that was one of my areas of expertise when I got my Ph.D. If I say to you that the majority of wealth building is psychological, that your mind contains the keys to your economic freedom and you refuse to believe me, then what you have effectively done is proven that everything I'm saying is true because what you have effectively done when you don't want to believe something is use your mind to take the keys to your freedom and throw them in the toilet.

Just as quickly as you can disengage with an idea, you can also believe it and watch it manifest and grow. This is not some wacky, make you feel good jargon. It is reality. Just conduct research on 5 different self-made millionaires and you will see consistent patterns emerge, especially the importance of growing one's wealth over time.

The same way I'm telling you that you could use your mind to free yourself from that cage, you can also ignore good information and advice. Just as your mind can unlock the door of the cage, you can use your mind to build a cage that you will never get out of. The same power that you have to free yourself is the same power you have to make yourself into a better slave.

Now I can't make you change your mind. As I have started before, I'm not trying to do any of that. I'm simply doing my best to share what I can that will help those of you who want to make a difference, who want to make a change and who want to get somewhere else to make a change. It really does start with psychology.

Most of the people who I know who are very successful, who become wealthy did so because they believed that it was possible and they poured into that possibility. They didn't fall for the whole victim mindset. What is the value in being a victim?

There's no good reason for you to just give up. Even if you don't have a chance to win, still try because at some point, there is still hope and there is still a tangible probability that your effort will pay off.

I cannot emphasize enough, the importance of studying this information carefully. You may find that you have to read this book more than once to truly grasp all of the information—that is perfectly ok. Gather up some of your friends and have a book study or a book club where you use the information in this book to assess what you are currently doing, process the information and set goals.

Take notes, write some things down, study this and remind yourself of these ideas if you run into any hurdles because, believe me, you will. Most successful people have experienced some level of failure before experiencing success. The key thing is to keep going. There is something to be said about the value of endurance and tenacity.

Remember, most things are very basic in terms of wealth building. Also, know that we have resources that are available to help you with the process. Go to: www.blackmoney103.com if you'd like to join our program on how to start a Black business. Also, if you would like to learn how to invest in the stock market, go to theblackstockmarketprogram.com.

The reason why I offer these programs and others in the Black Business School is because the road to wealth building is often shrouded in mystery. If you truly don't understand something, how can you even attempt to master it?

Some of you are already enrolled in our programs. Some of you haven't made the decisions yet, but I hope you will give it consideration because I will go pound for pound with any of the professors you had in college who charged you $40,000 a year. The faculty that we have are just as good as, and probably better than, the people you had. Most importantly, most of those faculty members weren't Black and did not focus only on the black community. We support and affirm Black students and their success—it's our specialty.

Whether it is because of this book and/or our various courses, I would just love for us to have millions of black people who really embrace the fundamentals of a wealth building or a Millionaire Mindset—not because we're on a paper chase and we want to drive Bentleys and ride on fancy yachts. That's fine if you want to do that. I'm sure yachts are very nice, but at the end of day, it's about the freedom.

It's about just doing whatever you want to do. And money is a conduit for doing that. I'm not here to tell you what you should want to do. I'm here to just say whatever it is, life is too short to be in a cage, so get out of the cage. Go live your life. The reality is that money helps you to do that. Teach your kids how to do the same thing. Don't be afraid to talk about money or wealth.

Create a set of three to four principles that you choose to live by. Just pick some rules that can govern your success. You don't have to memorize everything right off the bat. Instead, think, "Yeah, these are some things I want to keep in mind, that I'm going to hold onto that are going to remind me to change my habits."

It's not going to happen overnight. It takes time and that's fine. Don't let the hype of social media and popular culture convince you that the opposite is true.

Also, keep learning about wealth every single day of the week, talk about it, talk to family members about it, go read stuff, go read some books on it, read articles about it. Come hang out with me, I'll teach you some stuff. I teach all the time. That's what I love to do.

Once you have the information, what you do with it is up to you. Sure, a lottery ticket can make you an instant millionaire, but the odds are not in your favor. Why not engage in a wealth-building process that actually works to your advantage and is not dependent upon chance?

And remember, it all starts with how you think.

CHAPTER 4

UNDERSTANDING THE PURPOSE OF MONEY

You are probably familiar with the O'Jay's song "Money, money, money" or the scripture that "Money is the root of all evil". Or maybe you grew up watching *New Jack City*. Regardless of the context, black people have an interesting relationship with money. We tend to love it or blame it for all of our problems—neither extreme is particularly healthy, especially as it relates to thinking like a millionaire.

In fact, you may be asking, "Why are we talking about money and why are we talking about the purpose of money?"

A large part of the reason that we're talking about the purpose behind money is because a lot of people get the wrong information when it comes to what money means, what it should be used for and what you should do with it when you get it. If you watch TV, you'll see that a lot of people will get money and they will celebrate by going shopping and throwing it away and throwing it up at the club and doing all kinds of stupid things with it. Of course, I don't advocate any of this. What I do propose is that we have a healthier attitude when we think about the purpose of money.

Money is something that everybody wants. I mean everybody likes it. There's nothing with liking money. There's nothing wrong with using it for the things that are important to you. You just want to understand how to get it, how to keep it and how to use it in a productive way. Now, why do people want money?

Number one, money is power. People who have the most money in America tend to have the most power. They can do what they want. People kiss their butts. They're allowed to go and do whatever they want. They have freedom and they have access that is tied to their money. It may not be fair and it may not be right, but it is what happens in a society built on capitalistic ideas.

Freedom means that you can do what you need to do. If you don't like your job, you can quit your job. You can go get another job or you can build your own business or you can take the day off. A lot of people can't do that if they don't have money.

Additionally, money gives you flexibility. Flexibility means that if you don't like the neighborhood you live in, you're not trapped. You can move to a different neighborhood. If you don't like the car you drive, you can buy a new car. If you have relatives who need financial help, you're able to help them because you have the flexibility to make a loan or to support them or make an investment to help somebody else.

Money is also a form of security. When you don't have money, you worry. You get nervous and you're always wondering, "Oh my gosh. How am I going to get to the next paycheck or how am I going to get the next, whatever? How am I going to pay this bill and pay that bill?"

Let's be honest, a lot of people worry about money. Most people think about money every single day, all day long or at different parts of the day. Money is a constant worry for people so if you can get enough money to do what you want, then you have the security to really do what you want to do. It also offsets unnecessary stress and conflict in our households and in our communities.

Money can lead to a life of luxury. This is not inherently a bad thing. If you work hard and you save your money and you invest it properly and you want to get a Mercedes, buy yourself a Mercedes. The problem is that people will buy a Mercedes when they can't hardly afford anything else. They end up in financial trouble and they end up deep in debt because they're trying to buy stuff that they don't really need. Too often it is to impress others.

Another thing that money gives you is a form of exclusivity. Exclusivity basically means that you get to do stuff other people can't do. They have an old saying that says that you spend a few years living like nobody else will so that you can spend the rest of your life living like no one else can. Now, what does that mean?

It's like being in college and a friend says, "Oh, man. I don't want to study another two more hours. You're crazy. Let's go play Xbox or let's go outside or let's watch TV or let's do whatever."

You are the person who does what nobody else will. You put in that extra two hours of study or if you have a job, you work that extra two or three hours or if you have a dream, you spend a couple of extra hours building your dream because later, when everybody else says, "Oh, man. I can't. I want to go on vacation but I can't. I got to work." You get to go. You are in an exclusive space. Other people say, "Oh, man. I hate my job. I wish I could quit but I can't."

You say, "I hate my job and I'm going to quit because I got money in the bank. I'm good." Other people may say, "Oh, man. I can't eat at that restaurant or I can't afford that car because I'm just not doing well financially." You can go buy that car. You can go eat at that restaurant. You spend some years doing what nobody else will because now you can do what nobody else can.

I reflect on my own life and see how this actually rings true. I remember being in college and I can remember my girlfriend dumping me because I wanted to study so much. I wanted to study for long periods of time and she thought I was a nerd. Of course, like most girlfriends, she wanted to spend quality time with me. I get that, but what she didn't understand is that I had a vision of what I wanted and that required extra time and attention dedicated to my studies. Yes, I probably was a little bit of a nerd, but I had a dream.

I said, "One day, I want to live a good life because I've put in the work now and I have put myself ahead so that I can get what I want later on down the line."

Years later, a lot of those friends who made fun of me for studying all the time or who thought I was a little bit of a nerd said, "Man, I wish I had your life." I was thinking, "Well, you could have had my life if you wanted it, but you didn't want to do it. I was willing to do it, now I can do so many other things, but you weren't willing to do it. Now you cannot do this."

Some people may read that and think it sounds harsh, but it is not. We all make decisions that have implications for other decisions that we will make. I sacrificed certain relationships, partying, and other "fun" activities because I knew that it was just a matter of time before I could fully enjoy those things on my *own terms.*

Now, I'm not looking down on anyone; I wasn't talking poorly about them or anything like that, but I definitely thought about it and I said, "You know those things my mother told me about making the sacrifice early really made a big difference. Make that sacrifice early so that later on down the line, you can have the life that you want to have and you don't have to hate your life."

What does this have to do with money? Everything. Let's start by asking: What is money?

Let's start with the basics. Money is any circulating medium of exchange including coins, paper money, and demand deposits. What does that mean? That means that money is a way to represent value. From the time most of us are three years old and onward, we know what money is. You know that money can maybe buy you candy or money can get you the toy that you want or whatever.

Even kids know that money has value. Money is a way to represent value and people exchange it and give it to each other to create value. Now, the other thing about money is that money is powerful like fire. Fire can either be used for good or can be used for bad. Fire can cook your food and keep you warm, or it can burn you alive. Money ultimately is the same way. Money can be used for good things and money can be used for bad things, but just like anything that's very powerful, you have to know how to use that power in an intelligent way.

Now, here's a case study that I want you to consider. There are two professional athletes and I want you to think about how they used their money and I want you to tell me which one made the smarter decisions. The first athlete is named Vince Young. Vince Young was a professional football player. Vince Young had a $26 million-dollar contract when he first entered the NFL. Vince loved to play sports. That's all he thought about was sports, sports, sports. He didn't really talk about much else, at least not early on.

He, reportedly, spent $5,000 a week at the Cheesecake Factory. Now, $5,000 a week is a quarter million dollars-worth of food during a calendar year. He, allegedly, spent $600 to $1,000.00 on alcohol at the club. He bought fancy cars and expensive airline tickets. Now, obviously, this was his hard earned money and he could spend it as he saw fit.

I want you to tell me if that was a good or bad way to spend money. I want you to think about it: Good or bad? Also think about why/why not?

Here's my answer. It's bad. Vince spent $26 million in six years on things that did not make him money. There was no return on his investments. He did not own the restaurants, the clubs, or the car dealerships.

Simply explained, he put money out, and he didn't get any money back. Now, he's no longer in the NFL because he can't play football anymore or he can play but he's just not good enough. He thought football was going to take care of him for the rest of his life. In reality, football takes care of you for about three, four or five years. Now, he is bankrupt and is worth a negative amount of money.

The next example is Shaquille O'Neil. He's a former professional basketball player and entrepreneur. What did Shaq spend his money on? He spent $30,000 for a master's degree in business and then he spent $60,000 for a doctoral degree. He also bought 172 restaurants, 150 car washes, 40 fitness facilities and fancy cars.

I pose the same question: I want you to tell me if that was a good or bad way to spend money. I want you to think about it: Good or bad? Also think about why/why not?

It's very good. Shaq took the money that he made from basketball and he made that money worth more money. He invested it so now Shaq is rich. Not only is Shaquille going to be rich for the rest of his life but his children will be rich, his grandchildren will be rich, his great-grandchildren will be rich and his great, great-grandchildren will be rich and his great, great, great-grandchildren will be rich. 150 years from today, 200 years from now, Shaq will have family members who are living off of the hard work he did today. He did what nobody else would so that he and his family can live like nobody else can.

He planted a seed and that's the goal. You always want to plant a seed with your money so your money can grow. Don't turn around and just give your money back to the same people who just gave it to you in the first place.

Now, here's some ways money can be used for good. Number one save it. If you make $10, try to save $6 out of that 10 or at least half of your earnings. Don't spend more than you make.

Also, don't just sit on your money. Don't just spend it and don't just hold it. You want to invest it so you can invest money on an education; you can invest money on a small business;

you can invest money in somebody else's business where they're doing all the work and you're just collecting the pay. There are several diverse and innovative ways that you can invest your money.

Number three, invest in the people you love. This means give back to your community. Donate to organizations that you care about. Make sure that other people benefit when you give money, not just yourself. You're not put in this world to be a selfish person. If you think like a selfish person then you will have the problems and the spiritual weakness of a selfish person. Always be willing to support and give to the people who you love and the people you care about.

What else? Keep it. It means know the difference between what you want and what you need. If you go out and you see the Beats by Dre headphones and they cost $300 and you have a dream that you're saving for, you might want to get some less expensive headphones or save up for the Beats by Dre headphones but make sure you're saving for your future at the same time.

The best way to make money is from good investments. What's an investment? What does that mean? That's where you take money and you put it in to something and you get more money back. If I have a friend who starts a lemonade stand and he needs $20 to start his lemonade stand, then I might say, "Okay. I'll give you $20 to start the lemonade stand and you do all the work, but I want half of the money."

That means he's going to be out there all day serving lemonade and you don't have to do anything. You can work if you want and not work, but if you are the person providing the capital, you still get a cut of the money so each day if he brings home $10 a day from selling lemonade, you could say, "Well, where's my five bucks?"

Investing is a good way to make money. That's how I make most of my money. I make healthy investments now. I don't really like working as much. I still work, but I don't have to work; instead, I invest in things and in people. Again, money can lead to freedom.

Next, get paid to solve a problem or fulfill a need; this is the cornerstone of entrepreneurship. You should definitely learn how to have your own business even if you work for somebody else. The reason you want to have your own business is because companies that you go work for might decide one day that they don't need you anymore. They might fire you for no reason or you might be downsized. You may not be able to find a job or if you do have a job, you don't want to get all of your money from one place. You are running the risk that your financial stability is dependent upon someone else.

And, it might not be enough, especially as your life style changes. You might be making $500 a week and you might want to have $1,000 a week. If you've got a side business in addition to your job, then that means that you'll have that extra money to do the things that you want to do as opposed to just trying to sweat it out and get by, paycheck by paycheck.

I know too many people, college educated and otherwise, who are trying to make ends meet by living paycheck to paycheck when they don't have to. Again, it is a mindset.

Ask yourself: "What else can I do?" You want to choose a career that you love. A lot of people think that a job is something you pick just for the money. If they get a job offer and they're paid a lot of money to do the job, they'll take the job and won't think twice about it. I think that you should consider other variables like quality of life and work-life balance if that is important to you. A job is always more meaningful and enjoyable if you like what you do. Find something that you love.

And be realistic. I mean don't think that you're going to be like a professional basketball player or something if you're only five feet tall and you have never played an organized sport. Be intentional and find something that you love and try to turn that into your career. It is dangerous to enter into a job thinking, "Oh, I have to take the highest paying job."

Your happiness is the most valuable thing that you have and

you don't want to be in a situation where you're not happy in life.

As you think more about the purpose of money, think about Bill Gates. Yes, you read that correctly. Bill Gates makes all of his money from his investment. His money works for him. He has money invested in stocks. He has money invested in companies. He has money invested in his own company. He has a lot of money invested and he can live off of the interest alone from those investments.

Think about it this way, the money he's making from his investments makes more money in two days than Lebron James makes in an entire year. That's what it means to have your money working for you. Believe it or not, you could do the same thing or something similar. Maybe you won't have as much money as Gates but you want to be in a position where your money is working for you.

This leads to the question of: How can you keep your money? The first way you keep money is you want to have a realistic budget. This means that you want to know what you're going to spend your money on. For example, if you get $500 at the end of the week, you want to budget what you're going to do with that money. You don't want to just spend the money and throw it out there and not know where your money is going and why.

You want to have a budget and you want to stick to it. This will require discipline and self-control. In that budget, you want to make sure that whatever amount that you've received, that you're saving at least, 20 or 30% of that amount so that you can buy businesses later on or so you can make investments. In other words, you are working towards letting your money work for you because you made the right investments. But, you can't make the right investments if you don't have the initial capital to invest. Whether you are working for yourself or someone else, you should still be looking towards the future.

My advice is for you to spend a little and save a lot. When you're spending, don't feel like you have to keep up with other people. Now, I'm going to tell you a secret about the way people spend money, especially in the United States. Americans spend money like idiots. They throw their money away. They waste their money. They're constantly throwing it out in different directions and it's not good. That's why a lot of Americans are really struggling economically.

Too many Americans can't afford to pay the bills and that's because they let companies convince them that, "Oh, you have to get the latest iPhone or you have to buy this toy for your kids or you have to buy this car even though your other car is working perfectly fine". You want to ignore all of that. Don't spend up all of your money because you will end up broke or financially unstable.

Next, make your money work for you. I talked about this previously, but I want to re-emphasize it in a chapter that is about the purpose of money. Make investments. When your money is working for you and when you have it invested, it's a great feeling because you *own* something. For example, I talked to a young lady who likes to do hair.

She said, "I want to do hair and get paid to do it." I said, "How much do you want to get paid?" She said, "About $10, $12 an hour." I said, "Okay. That's not a bad idea, so let's say you get $12 an hour and you work 40 hours a week; you will make about $500 a week, something like that.

I said," Now, let's consider this other idea. Let's say, you learn how to have your own business and you have a hair salon and you have five chairs in the hair salon. Let's say that you don't even do the work. You just own the business, but you hire other young ladies or other young men who want to do hair; they do the hair for the customers. Let's say that the business makes $8,000 a week and it costs you $4,000 a week to pay all of your employees and overhead expenses, including utilities."

I asked, "Do you know that you get to keep that other $4,000 a week and you don't even have to do any work? You just get paid because you own the business."

When I said it like that, she says, "Wait a minute. You mean if I'm working my butt off, I would get the 500 a week but if I'm not working and I'm the owner, I can make 3, 4, $5,000 a week?" I said, "Yeah." She said, "Why would I make more money for doing less work?" I said, "That's how businesses work. That's why you want to run a business. That's why you want to be the boss."

If you paid the cost to be the boss, then you get a lot of the financial rewards from being the boss. It's not easy though. Being a boss means that sometimes it's risky and sometimes it's stressful. Sometimes you do have to work hard as a boss because your employees don't show up or you have to train them. You also have to work as hard as the people who work for you. It's not easy but you will love it more because it's your business. You're not working hard for somebody else's dream; you're working hard for your dream. You're working hard for the thing that you want and the thing that you believe in.

It's also important to grow your money. You get more money by creating wealth. Being wealthy is very different from being rich. Now let me say that again. Being wealthy is very different from being rich.

What's the difference between being rich and being wealthy. Number one, if you're rich, you get what they call instant gratification. That means that when you want something, you get it now. If you want to feel good, you feel good now. You can't put it off to the future because you want it right now. That's how people feel when they use drugs or get drunk or spend their money. They want to feel good right now. They don't want to save it for later, but the problem is that they may feel bad later on because they run out of money and then they're broke. They're like, "I'm broke. I don't have any money. Life is so hard for me."

You don't want to be one of those people. You want to be a person who believes in delayed gratification. Delayed gratification means that you still want to feel good. You're still going to get to enjoy your money and you're going to enjoy your life, but you are willing to wait if you have to.

Next, a rich person does not generate intergenerational wealth. What is intergenerational wealth? Intergenerational wealth is what Shaquille O'Neil generated where he doesn't just benefit from the money he makes, his children benefit, his grandchildren will benefit, his great-grandchildren will benefit, his great, great-grandchildren will benefit, his great, great, great-grandchildren will benefit and you get the point. It goes on and on and on. That's intergenerational where people after you're dead are still benefiting from what you did while you were alive.

People who are rich don't do that. They often think, "Oh, I get cash money. I'm going to go throw it up at the club. I'm going to go buy me a Lambo. I'm going to do this, do that." People who just think about getting money so that they can give it all away and spend it tend to be rich, but they are not wealthy. Those people don't generate intergenerational wealth. They don't really care about their kids like that. They're not taking care of their children and grandchildren. They're taking care of themselves today because they want instant gratification.

Wealthy people don't do that. Wealthy people generate wealth for the next generation. That's what you want to do. What else do rich people not do? Rich people don't like to give back to the community because they want to keep it all for themselves. They want to make sure they stay paid and everybody else stays broke. A wealthy person understands that when I benefit my family and my community, I'm also benefiting myself. That's very important.

What else do rich people do? Rich people spend money on things that depreciate in value. What does that mean? To depreciate in value means that something drops in value like a car. When you buy a car, it instantly starts to drop in value. Most cars are not going to be worth more money two years from now than what they are worth right now. When you buy a car, you're giving money away. It might be a nice car; it's fancy and even, top of the line, but it's not going to let you get to a place where your money is working for you. It is not designed to do that.

Wealthy people don't spend all their money on cars; they spend their money on assets or things that appreciate in value. For example, if you buy an apartment building and everybody in the apartment building is paying rent to you, that building is going to go up in value and you're going to get all of the rent money from all of the people who are living in your building. If you buy a business, that tends to go up in value. If you buy real estate, a house or land, that appreciates in value.

You buy stocks and bonds and they also go up in value. Some types of jewelry go up in value. You want to buy things that are going to go higher in value and not things that go lower in value. Rich people are more likely to end up in bankruptcy. Bankruptcy is when the amount that you owe, or your debts, are higher than your assets and the amount that you have. You see a lot of very rich people, a lot of rich entertainers and athletes, in particular, go broke. In fact, it is estimated that 75% of all professional athletes go bankrupt within 5 years of the time that they stop playing.

They make millions of dollars over the course of their athletic careers, but most of them go bankrupt. Wealthy people don't tend to end up in bankruptcy because they protect themselves against that. What else? Rich people have limited streams of income. What does that mean? A stream of income is where you get your money from so if you have a job, you have one steam of income. If you have, two jobs, you have two streams of income. If you have four businesses, you have four streams of income.

Rich people are thinking, "Oh, I get one good job. I'm making good money from my one job and I get one stream of income so I'm doing good." Wealthy people don't think that way. Wealthy people have multiple streams of income. Most wealthy people that I know will have several businesses. All of them are paying them money. They get in a situation where they say, "Okay. I got 5,000 a month coming from this business. I got 10,000 a month coming from that business. I got 8,000 a month coming from that business." They have multiple streams of income and this is important because you're usually earning more money that way. It's better to have five people paying you than just one.

Number two, you are more likely to be protected in case one of your situations goes bad. If you have one job and one stream of income, then if that company goes bankrupt or they fire you, then you're going to be struggling. You might say, "Oh my God. I can't find a job. What am I going to do?" If you have multiple streams of income, you can say, "Okay. You know what, that stream of income dried up. I'm not making money from that but I'm making good money from other streams so I'm going to be good."

Next, rich people tend to have to work for their money for life. Wealthy people tend to let their money work for them. If you think about an athlete or even a lawyer or a doctor, some of those people think that they're going to make money by working until they're old and gray. A wealthy person actually says, "I'm going to keep saving and investing my money into businesses so then later on I don't have to work anymore. My money is going to work for me."

Now, let's look at a couple of case studies on wealth versus riches. On one hand, example A, we have the rapper named 2 Chainz. On the other hand, we have a young brother that I'm going to tell you about shortly. 2 Chainz often raps about buying new cars. He's worth about $2 million. He has no other known stream of income other than rap and maybe a couple of endorsements and stuff like that but not a whole lot. Is he wealthy enough? To answer this honestly, probably not. Why? Because 2 Chainz spends a lot of his money on cars and jewelry and he has just one source of income.

Here's example B. This is more realistic portrait of black wealth. Most of us are not going to get chance record deals or become rappers.

Jaylen Bledsoe is his name. Jaylen Bledsoe is just 16 years old and he's an entrepreneur. He lives in St. Louis. He owns a technology firm. He employs 113 contractors. His company is worth $3.5 million.

Even though he is a teenager, he will never *have to* work at McDonald's or Burger King or anything else. Is Jaylen wealthy? Absolutely. Jaylen contributes to his community by hiring people.

He's not out begging for a job; instead, he's creating jobs. He also has built a business that he can pass on to his children, so not only is he a millionaire, but his children and grandchildren will be millionaires because of the seeds that he's planted today. He's letting his money work for him. He's not doing all the work. He's got 113 contractors who are doing the work and he only has to work to make sure that they are doing what he's telling them to do.

Now, here's the summary. Always strive to put money to good use. Don't waste it. Always budget and save your money. Always aim to build wealth, not just riches. You are meant to be great. You are meant to be wealthy. You are meant to be intelligent and don't let anybody tell you differently.

CHAPTER 5

SUSTAINING WEALTH 101

What does it mean to build wealth? How does one build wealth? How can you attain financial security? This chapter was born out of a simple conversation that went as follows:

> "Are you financially secure?"
>
> "No! I'm not financially secure, and black people can't be financially secure 'cause we don't own anything!"

I wish that this conversation was atypical, but it happens with great frequency. So much so that perpetuating this idea is irresponsible. We, as black people, have a misconception of what financial security actually looks like.

Financial security is very important, and let me tell you why it matters and why most Americans don't have it. The big problem we have in America is that there's this really interesting intrigue factor as it relates to designer and luxury items. There are a lot of people who want to live like the Kardashians. I really think reality T.V. plays a significant part in shaping our belief systems.

Reality T.V. creates a false reality—it's ironic that they call it reality T.V., but it's not reality. It's actually a false reality that leads people to want to live in luxury. Everybody sees what's happening on these shows, and the way those so-called wealthy people live, and everybody wants to get that stuff.

Black people watch shows like *Love & Hip Hop*. And we see these rappers—and I know a lot of the rappers—and we idolize their leisurely, yet luxurious lifestyles.

I've been on The Breakfast Club three times. I'm going back there soon. Being in the public light puts you in certain spaces where you can see behind the curtain. It's like a "Wizard of Oz" game. And I said, you know, people just don't know the reality behind all of this. They really think that these people on T.V. have as much money as they pretend to have. And so, my goal is to kind of blow the lid off of the whole thing, and just say it's all a lie and it's all a myth. It's not real. It's not real!

We have to be honest because this influences how wealth and money are often defined on our communities.

Now, I'm not saying that there's not some money floating around and I'm not saying that they aren't making big deals. They might go on the road and make $50,000 a night, $100,000 a night, or whatever. But the problem is that making $100,000 a night doesn't mean anything if you're spending $90,000 a night. Logically, if you're giving all of your money away and it goes through your hands, it means nothing if you're not doing anything to preserve your money.

Having a million dollars in the bank for a short period of time does not mean nearly as much as having that money in the bank for a long period of time. So, where we get it wrong is that we think that people that make a lot of money are automatically doing well. And that's just not true. Some of the most financially distressed people in this country are the ones who have the best jobs. They're the ones who have the most money because that leads many of them down the path where they are living a certain lifestyle that they cannot afford to impress a bunch of people who don't even matter.

You are trying to live a Facebook life where you're getting on

Facebook, taking a picture with your Mercedes-Benz, and saying "I'm so blessed; I was just so blessed."

You ever see that? Where somebody is doing their humble brag, where they're talking about how blessed they are, and they really want to brag about the new Mercedes they just bought. Well, what they don't show you is that America's going deeper in debt in order to do that. (I am going to talk about that in greater detail in this chapter).

First, CNBC says that one in eight Americans is willing to take on $1,000 or more in debt to depict an extravagant lifestyle, according to a recent study. Now, one in eight is not a huge number, but there are a lot of people who are going deep in debt for things that don't always make a lot of economic sense. Luxury items are in a category and as of late, even a college education has fallen into that category because it is so expensive and many people cannot pay that much for it.

Remember, everything should have a price. And there should be a point to where you say, you know, I think I want that, but I don't want to pay that price for it. Education is now in that category because it really shouldn't cost you forty, fifty-thousand dollars a year to go to school. But because we feel that it's mandatory, we feel like we have to do it.

People don't realize that you have to be creative about how you move forward in the wealth game. It's just like companies. Some of the biggest companies in the world that make the most money are bad investments because they are borrowing too much to get what they need.

So, it's as if you were say to me, "Hey I'm hungry Boyce." I say, "Okay. You should eat some food." You say, "Absolutely, I agree." And I say, "Okay, well to get a meal-- and I know you're hungry, I know you want to eat, you said my food is good-- so, to eat here, it's going to cost you $1,000 a plate." Well, I mean, you would probably be within your right to give me the finger and cuss me out. Understandably, you would say well, "I love Dr. Boyce's fried chicken, but it's not worth $1,000 a plate."

One of the fundamental rules of finance is that you have to

know what the price is. What is your price? How far are you willing to go to obtain that bank? Often, when it comes to luxury items, whether it is education or things we feel like we need, we get to a point where there is no such thing as a price that is too high. However, I think that you should try to avoid that mindset.

Additionally, Americans are not saving. 28% of Americans have nothing in their savings account. Nothing. That is the epitome of economic vulnerability. If you are in that category, don't be ashamed. But you have to fix that. Life happens. Or, things break down. Things go wrong and crises emerge all of the time, so you want to be proactive as opposed to reactive.

People who tend to get ahead financially are proactive people. Proactive means that you don't just react to the crisis that happened yesterday; you are prepared for the crisis that might happen tomorrow. Proactive thinking is not popular in the black community.

There, I said it. I said it. Get mad at me. But proactive thinking and planning are simply not popular in the black community. You know what's popular in the black community? Let me tell you what's popular in the black community. What's popular in the black community is to live life on the edge or on the brink of economic destruction, and then cry, scream, holler, go crazy, and pray to Jesus when the economic calamity has occurred. When you could have prepared yourself.

The best example of this is funerals. How many times have you seen a funeral where the family is devastated financially and cannot afford to bury the person who just died? So, they go to church, and they're begging the church to take up a collection plate to help them bury Uncle Willy. Well, the whole family is in complete chaos because Uncle Willy didn't spend $30 a month on some life insurance. But, here's the thing. You might say, Uncle Willy couldn't afford life insurance. But, I saw Uncle Willy go to McDonald's every other day. I saw Uncle Willy spend money on liquor, weed, and sneakers. I saw Uncle Willy spending money to go to the movies.

So, why is it that Uncle Willy had an easier time spending

money on things that added no economic value to his family and to his legacy, but people have a problem when you're talking about paying for something that's a necessity.

Well, the reason is that people don't really seem to want to do the dirty work. They don't really want to handle necessities. Necessities are boring. People tend to aim for the extravagant. They enjoy saying, "Look at the new car I bought. I got the Chrysler, it looks just like a Bentley." Or, "Look at the outfit I got, I look so fly tonight." And so there's that sort of instant gratification or desire to look good as opposed to actually being good and being in a good position. That's very prevalent and popular. It's not natural; instead, it is marketed consistently to our communities.

I'll give you another example. A lot of people go in debt because they are really trying to keep up with the Kardashians. They watch Kim Kardashian and her family. They read about what they're making, 100 million dollars a year, with this empire they've built. And they watch the Kardashians, and everybody wants to be like the Kardashians and so they go in debt trying to be like the Kardashians.

Well, here's the interesting thing about that Kardashian lifestyle. Kim Kardashian and many of the family members admit to altering their appearances. In other words, they pay to look a certain way. If they were not born with it, they buy it.

So, a lot of us, in a way, can be compared to Kim Kardashian. We have that instant gratification mentality. That mentality that says I can just buy what I want; therefore, I'm just going to do what's best for me now and not really think about the consequences.

I encourage you to find a way to understand that if your desire is truly to look good, if you really want to look good, there's nothing wrong with that, but I really encourage you to also find a way to be in a good financial position while you do it. To not ruin yourself and ruin your future and sacrifice your future in order to have what basically amounts to instant gratification. That's all it is. It's just the desire to have everything now, now, now.

21% of Americans don't even have a savings account, and 70% of Americans are in debt. 30% have no plans to pay off the debt. So, a large number of Americans are not only going to die without any wealth, a large percentage of Americans are going to die in the hole. They're going to die leaving a legacy of debt. And that's a very scary thing because when you talk about death, death is scary. Death is already traumatizing to the people you love, and to add debt to that just compounds the anguish.

Here's a couple of rules of thumb. First, when it comes to financial security, just know this: Let's get this out of our heads about this whole thing about how much money somebody makes. Who cares how much money somebody makes? Earning money is not the key to financial security. It is having more money that can make a difference. It is keeping the money that you get that matters. It is what you hold onto that makes all the difference.

That's why some Jewish refer to black people as liquid money. This old Jewish man once said, "Yeah, you know, we call the African-American community liquid money." You know how liquid flows through your hands, if I take this water and I pour it in my hands-- it's going flow through and land all over my pants, that's why I didn't pour it out. But liquid money-- the fact that we're seen that way should be an absolute insult to all of us.

Now, everybody's not going to change. Here's what I predict. The black community, at large, will maintain some of its very bad habits. The bad habits of our community are, one, we don't pick up books as much as we should. Two, we watch more T.V. than other groups of people, that's why they build entire T.V. networks off of our sluggishness—or our desire to be intellectually sluggish. We use social media more than other people do, so a lot of people build their economic success off of the backs of black people. That's not going to change.

What can change, is you. What can change is you. In my house, we don't think this way. In my house, we embrace the idea of economic intelligence. In my house, we preserve wealth, and we build wealth, because the wealth that you build becomes your protection. It protects your dignity; it protects your family; and it protects your sanity. There's a lot of black people who are really going crazy because they're out here begging and it effects their physical and mental health because they're worried about money.

It is true that America is still going to be a capitalist society, and people are going to be stressed out about money. I think the question that we must ask ourselves as parents—and I'm a parent too, and I ask myself this question—is: Do I really want my kids to be stressed? Or do I want my kids to be strong? Do I want my kids to be stressed, or do I want them to be blessed? You can bless your kids by planning, and making very basic steps to create financial security that lasts a long time.

I'll tell you a little secret. My daughter is big on hair and fashion and beauty and makeup, and we hold daddy/daughter business strategy meetings where we talk about her business, her product lines, and we talk about marketing. We also talk about distribution. We talk about monetization, inventory, processes, and I make sure that she knows how to keep her house in order economically.

As I tell her, I also tell you: Money isn't the only solution to the financial security question. What you're actually trying to do is not just get money; you're trying to build wealth. Wealth can be money, but wealth is not always money. And that's very important to understand, too. So, if you obtain some wealth, like you have a business and you have some assets, and you maybe have a brand name that you want to protect, you want to protect it and sustain it.

All of these things can be put into your trust when you die. I know that the name Dr. Boyce Watkins is a multi-million-dollar asset that I can leave to my children, and it is in my will and in my trust with my estate planning lawyer. This is how I want it to be preserved, and this is how I want the revenue to be doled out. Just like I did, you can do all of that for your heirs.

In terms of your goal, of what you want with your family, I'm really encouraging black people to build empires. You came from kings and queens, and you will, at some point, become kings and queens again. It's up to us to decide how quickly we want to accelerate the process. And the ability to be a king, or the ability to be a queen, really comes down to thinking like a king or a queen. A king or queen is not into foolishness. A king or queen is not easily swayed by the nonsense going on in the world. A king or a queen is a leader and not a follower. A king or a queen is able to build their house, and to defend that house.

So, what I would encourage you to do is think like a king or a queen, even if you don't have much. Pride is really important. Being proud of what you have is more important than the amount of what you have. You may not have a whole lot, but being proud of that and preserving that will make all the difference. And then, it gives you the opportunity to go in for the kill and to accumulate wealth. You must protect what you have to begin that process of building more, and then you'll have more to protect.

Now how can you protect against financial insecurity? Here are a few symptoms that will help you identify whether or not you might be a candidate for financial insecurity-itis. Number one, getting all of your income from one job is problematic. A lot of people think they're secure, but they're not. They lose that job and they're done. If you wake up every day stressed out because you might lose that job, then understand that you're stressed out for a reason.

Next, being deep in debt is a concern. Too much debt is the devil. Debt, and the over-accumulation of debt has become a huge problem for Americans. You want to be cautious about debt. I'm going to give you some rules on when you should and should not consider debt.

Not having a savings is also an issue. You save your money so your money can save you. A lot of people don't save at all; they don't understand the purpose of savings which is why they don't do it. Not investing can lead to financial insecurity. Your investments are where you're preserving capital to give yourself financial security, and it also gives your money an opportunity to work for you. People who are at the highest levels often have investment capital.

I recently read about big companies like Amazon. The founder of Amazon, Jeff Bezos, made 3.3 billion dollars yesterday. He literally made 3.3 billion dollars in a day, because of this company, Amazon, that he's been building for many, many years. And Amazon is a company you could have invested in, back in the year 2000 for as little as $5, $6, $7, $8 a share. Now, it's up to almost $1,000 a share. There are other *Amazons* out there; there are other companies out there that can allow your wealth to grow. But if you don't invest, then your money never gets a chance to grow.

Also, we don't have alternative streams of income. If you've only got one source of income, and you don't have any alternatives out there, then you're going to put yourself in a bad financial situation. You're in a risky scenario. You don't have financial security, in my opinion. No assets. The question is, what are your assets? What have you put your money in to that you could actually sell, if times get tough? Things that can generate additional revenue?

Lack of insurance is another indicator of financial insecurity. A lot of people are in financial turmoil because they didn't take the time to get adequate insurance. I say if you've got kids and you don't have life insurance, you don't love your kids. Unless you are just absolutely so destitute that you can't afford a $10 a month policy or $30 a month, that's a dollar a day, policy. Otherwise, it is inexcusable. But if you are buying anything other than life insurance, if you are going to Starbucks once a month or if you are buying a new pair of shoes once every month or two or if you can afford to go to the movies, then you should have adequate life insurance for your heirs.

Go back over many of these things and see where your gaps or weak spots are. As you become more financially secure, let's mark them off of the list and celebrate your milestones, no matter how small. Let's make sure that we address these issues. You're not going to rectify them overnight though, you have to give yourself time.

You can start now by creating multiple streams of income. Now, that's easier said than done. I'll give you a personal example. In my own company, somebody might come up to me and say, "Hey, Dr. Boyce. This was a great month, look at how much money we made over here." I think, *what happens if that faucet turns off*? I'm not thinking about how much money we have now; I'm thinking about what's going to happen if that source gets shut down. So, first thing I think about when I accumulate anything is, *how do we defend that*? Well, one way you defend it is through diversification.

When you're celebrating because cousin Pookie got that good job with the law firm, he should be thinking about that next step of putting himself in a position where he's got income coming in from multiple sources, so he can preserve the lifestyle that he's grown accustomed to. So, I encourage you to have family conversations about how you can get some other little streams of income. Streams of income have to be grown; they're not easily acquired overnight because it takes time. New streams of income start off small and they often start off very sloppy. Most entrepreneurial families get it wrong the first time or two. That's why consistent education is really important.

In fact, right now my company is in the process of seeking to acquire property all across the country to set up economic empowerment centers so that people can gather every Saturday, just like at church, and talk about what they're trying to do and their economic journey, so that we can support each other. We need gathering spots because they will allow us to have conversations with other like-minded people, so we can build family empires.

I also encourage you to start with your own family and have regular conversations about developing multiple streams of income. This is a financial risk that you cannot bear if you are black in this country. A lot of black people are enslaved because of the fact that they are dependent on other people to pay their bills. And that's a vulnerability that you don't want to live with your whole life because it'll stress you out.

Furthermore, start thinking carefully about debt. Debt has gotten many Americans into trouble. Millions of Americans are drowning in debt. Most of the debt is stupid debt, or bad debt. Bad debt is debt that you take on for just any reason. Debt you take on to go out to eat, debt you take on to look like Kim Kardashian, debt you take on to go on vacation, debt you take on to buy the fancy new car when you could have got a good used car.

What I would also say, though, is that, in a way, when I think about spending, I think of heavy spending. I'm not one to tell you that you can't spend heavily, I'm just one to tell you that it's very, very important to avoid the mistake of not taking care of the fundamentals before you spend heavily. So, if you're going to go spend, make sure that you have your savings and investments in line before you go enjoy your money.

It's like food. There's nothing wrong with eating ice cream or chocolate cake, in my opinion; if eating chocolate cake was a crime, then I deserve life in prison because I will eat some chocolate cake all day long. But here's what I won't do: I won't eat chocolate cake before I've eaten the main course, or eaten my vegetables and all of the healthy food first. And I am not going to eat an entire chocolate cake because that would be gluttony. The same is true for excessive spending.

And so, what you see in America when it comes to money and the way people manage their money, are forms of economic gluttony. You see people just spending until they have nothing left, and all the money they spend is on stuff that doesn't matter, and then they go deep in debt to buy more stuff that doesn't matter, and then the banks are building wealth and you're just languishing away. So, don't let that be you.

Next, find a way to get out of the paycheck to paycheck scenario. You can get away from the paycheck to paycheck situation in a few ways. First of all, have long-term savings plans. If you can't save a lot of money now, save something. You can actually save more than you think, and let me tell you why I know you can save.

Think of anything that you spend $10 a day on. Over time that accumulates into significant money. So, what baffles me and what I find quite fascinating is how many people say they really cannot afford to save, when actually you have been a bank account, you have been an ATM machine for somebody else. You have served as a savings vehicle for people who have taken the money that you gave them, and they've put it into financial assets. They've put it aside for their family.

So, long-term savings can make a difference. Other streams of income can help you stop living paycheck to paycheck. So, when you have free time, you know, relax, take your naps, and recover from work, because work is tough, think of what else you can do. But always think about ways that you can make extra money. Don't feel that getting a job is enough. A lot of people will say, "I need money, I'm going to go find a job." Then they go find a job, and they might feel like they've handled their financial problem. Okay, now I've got a job, I'm doing good. Well, you're doing good, until you don't have a job anymore, right? So that means you're not really doing that good, because you're very vulnerable to actions that are outside of your control.

So, while you're in the security of having a job, you should say to yourself, "Okay, I'm going to live below my means and I'm going to take that last little 10%, or whatever, and I'm going to start putting it toward initiatives that will help me to really get financial security". This will help you get off the plantation, help me stop living paycheck to paycheck. Whatever it is so that you can be in a position where you are economically strong.

There are many of us who only respond to economic emergencies. We only respond when times get hard, that's when we get serious. That's when we want to learn. There are people that when I talk to them about economic security or economic intelligence, I know people, I see people, whether it's on social media or elsewhere, who only listen to me when they're broke. They only listen to me when they're scared. When you're broke and scared, I don't know what I can do to help you. Because you're in the middle of the fire. Your well-being, your good situation, clogged up your ears. But, don't let it.

And I can just think about that, think about a relative I had who was kind of like that. When he was doing well with money, you couldn't tell him anything. He was very confident; he was very bold, and very brash. And then, when the crisis would hit, he would turn into a little boy: "I didn't expect this to happen. I'm so sorry. I wish. . . I just need some help!" All of a sudden, he called me right back because he thought that I was the person who was going to give him the money that he needed.

And I think that is a reflection of that very reactive thinking that you see from a lot of people. And I encourage you to get away from that.

So, when you're doing well, that's the time when you prepare for the possibility that you might not be doing so well. When the sun is out, that's when you go buy an umbrella. Don't wait until it starts raining to buy an umbrella because you're going to get wet, and there may not be any umbrellas left to buy because everybody will be buying an umbrella when it starts raining.

Additionally, ownership of property gives you an economic cushion. When you own property and you own assets that appreciate in value, that gives you something that you can hold onto, something you can borrow against, maybe even sell, in case you run into what is called a liquidity problem. Liquidity is when you just need cash.

The next thing I encourage you to do is to repeatedly go through the concepts. Some of the concepts in this chapter and in this book are not going to make sense to you the first time you read them. But that's okay. If you read them over and over and over again, they will sink in. And have regular conversations about money that go beyond the typical conversations. Ask: How do we take the money that we have and create security as opposed to spending that money? How do we make sure that we are positioned economically with economic intelligence so we know how to identify opportunities when they arise?

A lot of people feel that there are no opportunities, not because there are none. They feel that there are no opportunities because they have never been taught to identify the opportunities. Think about fine jewelry, or antiques. If you put an antique in front of me, it could be literally worth a million dollars, and I wouldn't even know. If you come to me and you say, "I've got this ancient Romanian vase," or some crap, whatever. And, "I want you to buy, Dr. Boyce. I'm going to sell it to you for $50,000." I'm going to say no, I'm not going to buy that thing, it's ugly. It's old, it's rusty. But if I am educated on antiques, then I might jump at that and say, oh my god look at how much money I can make.

So, the ability to see opportunities comes from education. That's why we must educate ourselves, and we must educate our own. That's why we created theblackbusinessschool.com, if you want to go take a look at some of the other stuff we have. That's why we created theblackhistoryschool.com because we believe that black people should be teaching black people black history. So, I think that if you do that, if you educate yourself, you're going to know where the opportunities lie.

When you get a dollar, you want to ask yourself one very important question: How can I get this dollar to work for me? Tax refund, tax season is a great example of that. Where people get their tax refund, and they become an immediate stimulus package for the local mall downtown. The Arabs and the Greeks and the Chinese and everybody else that's sitting in the black communities, they are waiting for you to get your tax refund because you have partnered with them in your own economic exploitation. You have already made extremely detailed plans of how you are going to allow them to economically rape you once you receive that money.

It's not like they're fooling you into it, they're not tricking you into spending that money. They're not even asking you to do it. You, because you don't see the fertility of your money and the possibilities of your money, have willingly asked them to economically ruin you and to take everything you've got. And so, a person who becomes economically intelligent, who understands financial fertility, would say, "Okay, I got this $3,000 tax refund, and I'm in a bad situation. This money is helping me get out of my bad situation. Now, I could use this money to give me a temporary remedy for my bad situation, or I could use this money to get me a permanent remedy for my bad situation."

It all comes down to whether or not you think like an investor. Investors understand financial fertility, and financial fertility is where automatic millionaires come from. Many millionaires in America are not people who were born rich. They are not people who won the lotto. They are not people who got rich quick. They were people who got rich slowly, through automatic investments over a long period of time that allowed the wealth accumulation process to occur.

Ask yourself: What do I own? How many times do you really see our people, sitting around and really talking about what we own, instead of talking about how much money we make? Or what kind of fancy things we have? I got this car, oh those are nice boots. Whatever, right? How often do you really hear people talking about what they actually own? When I talk to my daughters about picking a man who is financially secure, I just tell them, look, if the man doesn't have a plan, don't get with him. If he isn't working hard to build that plan, don't get with him. Of course, he may not have assets today, but he's got to, at least, have an investor mentality where he's investing time to build something for the future.

And that's just the old-school in me; that's just basic fundamental stuff. There was a 94-year-old lawyer who just died and practiced law until he was 90. He made millions of dollars in the process. And he tells this funny story about how he met his wife. And he told his wife, he said, "Look. I just want you to know ..." -- this is like, 1942 or something, right? So, he says, "I just want you to know, that I would like to date you. I would like to pursue you. But I have to confess, I don't have much money now. However, I am working hard, I am educating myself, and one day I'm going to have plenty of assets and a lot of wealth, and I am going to take very good care of you." And so, she ended up marrying him; he kept his promise, and that's what happened.

And there's a part of me that just loves stories like that because I think that's kind of a basic, meaningful way for people to interact. And also, if you think about that, that's an investment decision. Because she's deciding, do I want to invest my life in this man? Do I want to attach myself to this ship? Do I want to draft this player to be on my team, or do I want to go along with somebody else? So, a lot of times, in relationships you're making an investment. You're taking a huge risk. And if you take that risk, or you invest in the wrong person, you can end up being devastated.

Just as relationships and partnerships are critical, so is ownership. It has to become part of our culture. It has to become part of our standard dialogue as a community. We must talk about owning things and not always talk about buying things. We have to talk about owning things and not just talk about how much money you make. We have to talk about ownership and not just complain about what other people own. Because at the end of the day, you can complain all day about the Arabs and the Jews and the Asians that are in your community, robbing you and selling you bad or crappy things at the corner store, but remember that they achieved an economic position that you could have also accomplished yourself.

You could also have owned those corner stores; you also could have come together as a family and put your money together and bought an asset that's making you money. You also have the right, as an American, to sell things. Now, you're not going to sell in their neighborhoods; they're not going to let you do that. And really, honestly, some would say that maybe we as black people shouldn't let them sell in our neighborhoods. But I think at the end of the day, complaining doesn't really get us what we want. It's really *actually doing* that's going to make the difference.

Ownership has to be premiere. If you want to start with ownership, start by owning a share stock. You can go buy share stock in five minutes. Just go, if you're in Black Money 102, if you're in the stock market investing program, then you have already bought stock, most likely. So, you are an owner. Now that you're owning things, now own more. Accumulate a little more.

And get in that habit.

Here's one of the best things that helped me a lot when I started thinking about wealth building. I got into the habit of owning things and accumulating assets, I got really addicted to that. I used to be a spend-aholic when I was younger, before I really started thinking about my financial future. I used to spend money. That was my weakness. And what I found was that, when I became an investor, I was still kind of a spend-aholic. I still pushed money around a lot, to the point where my brother gets very nervous.

The difference though, now, is that the money I spend is going into my business. So, the more I spend, the stronger my company gets. The more I spend, the more I own. You understand? So ultimately, find some way to keep doing what you're doing, but just think a little deeper about how you're doing it. If money burns a hole in your pocket and you like to spend it, then get together with your family and take that money, put it someplace where you can go and actually make money from that. Then what will happen is, you'll get even more money and you can make bigger investments, and it's just really a fun process.

So, think about ownership. Another step toward ownership is real estate. A lot of people tell me they can't buy a house, and I think that's so funny, because people don't understand that, mathematically, if you've rented property for twenty years, you've actually probably technically bought your landlord a house. You've actually bought a house; you just gave it away to somebody else. If you rent for thirty years, you probably bought them two houses. In fact, the economic system is very interesting in the sense that you have people who are able to build empires with other people doing all the work. It's very fascinating to see how that works.

And then, obviously, owning your own business is critical. I think a family that has those three things: 1) stocks and bonds, 2) real estate, and 3) a business will have some financial security because you're going to have assets and you're also going to have income from multiple sources. Your family should be a business. Your family is a business. That is your first business. If you m2ess that business up, then it makes it harder to do anything else. But if you do it right, then my god you will experience a type of heaven that you didn't think was even possible. You will experience a pride that will make you feel like you are King Jaffe Joffer from *Coming to America*.

I swear, I kid you not, but I love being able sit at the table as the patriarch of the Watkins family empire. And when my children get out of line, I do my James Earl Jones. "No, you will NOT disobey me!" I'm kidding, I don't do that. But I do actually like the idea of feeling like a king. I like the idea that my mother is elevated in a certain way, and we can do things for her. I also confess, I chose not to, I didn't get married. I know some of you all think that means I'm a bad person.

Now, I have a relationship with an awesome woman, and in my mind, I get to say to myself, yes, she is a queen, and she gets the security of being next to a man who has his masculinity intact. I love that. And I'm getting personal here, and I'm not trying to tell you all of my business, but that's the honest to God truth. I love the fact that our family endowment—we have a pile of capital, a pile of wealth, and a pile of assets—allows us to create jobs for our children, jobs for their friends, and jobs for relatives.

Most of my daily business doesn't involve responding to a boss. It involves being a boss. It involves having interesting conversations about possibilities. Today, I was sitting on the phone, and I was negotiating with someone about making a movie. And I said no, the budget's not going to be that much; it's going to be this much, and no, I need him to make sure he gets this done in this way. And I'll just tell you the truth, it makes life a lot more fun. And you never really completely are totally devoid of any economic risk. There's always something that can rattle the ship, but it's better to be on a bigger ship, and it's much more fun to own the ship.

I encourage you to figure out how to get you a ship, and own the ship. And that's what I teach. That's what we do in The Black Business School. I'm not really big on teaching you how to go and cater to white supremacy so you can get a better job. I'm just not good at that. If you come to me and you have trouble with your boss, and you come talk to me and you get advice from me, you better not do, it because I'm the guy that will get you fired. I will get you fired. Because I'm going to tell you, well, that doesn't make any sense. Why can he get away with calling you that? Or, that's wrong, why would they treat you that way? No, I don't think you should tolerate that.

So, I'm not the guy to talk to about how to keep a job. What I am, is, I'm the guy that will teach you where empires come from. And why everybody can have one. And empires don't have to be big. It's all about mindset. It's all about mindset. Is my empire the biggest empire on the block? No, it's not. I mean, it is worth a few million dollars. But even if you rewind and go back to when it was worth a few thousand dollars, I still drew a tremendous amount of pride by knowing that my family had something that belonged to us. That we had something that will be around, that the great-grandkids can talk about. Something that gives you pride.

Unfortunately, as black people, we lack pride sometimes. We don't feel any shame in begging. We have a lot of black men who are broken, who don't really understand that there's certain kinds of behavior that you should be ashamed of as a man. It's hard to be proud as a man when you're out begging for money, but there are a lot of guys who can do it, and I don't understand that. The tap-dancing to get into professional sports leagues because you didn't learn how to create any other economic or educational opportunities for yourself, that's something you should be ashamed of. You shouldn't be proud of that, you shouldn't be proud of catering to, and begging, people who historically hated you, and who don't respect you, to take care of you. There's no pride in that.

So, I didn't mean to go off on that tangent, but I think that ownership piece is really important. There are psychological studies that show that people who own something feel proud of it. They take good care of it. So, find something that you own, and be proud that it's yours. I don't care if it's a $5 share stock.

Another step in the financial security process is check your dang insurance. Make sure your insurance is intact. So many of us are under-insured, and when you actually get something worth losing and you don't insure it properly, you're asking for tragedy. Anytime there's a tragedy, anytime there's a calamity in my life or the lives of anybody else, the first question I ask myself is, could this have been avoided? Could this have been avoided? And let me tell you this. When it comes to black people, I would argue that the vast majority of things that happen to us when it comes to wealth and when it comes to health, could have been avoided.

If you look at why black people die, we don't die for the same reasons that white people die. White people die, honestly, from genetic hereditary stuff that they usually can't avoid so much. Because, honestly, I think that we have something genetically that makes us very, very strong. That's why people are afraid of us. Black people, unfortunately, will die from things like gunshot wounds which are avoidable. Heart disease, diabetes and a lot of aliments come from grandma's fried chicken. Or we are extremely obese and not even thinking about going to the gym, right?

And again, there's a mindset that was built that led to those sorts of decisions. It's not always our fault; we've been brainwashed. We have been conquered and brainwashed. That's why the black man is on his knees right now in America. It is because he's been brainwashed to live on his knees.

And so, what I have to encourage you to do, is to question everything. You must question everything in terms of how you were taught to live, how you were taught to think about money, and how you were taught to respond to things. I think that, for example, proactive versus reactive thinking is huge. The reason is that we have reactive thinking, where we respond to tragedies, but we don't prepare to prevent tragedies, that reactive thinking goes to the highest levels. Dr. Claud Anderson, in the book "Black Labor, White Wealth," speaks extensively about how black leadership is flawed, because many of our leaders only react to crises, because we think that being black means always being in a state of crises. It means you're always in a state of emergency. It means your world's always falling apart, it means you're always playing struggle-nomics and you'll never get a chance to play power-nomics.

So, the leadership is thinking this way, which trickles down to the people. So, my belief is that, you, being a black leader--because if you have children, you're a black leader, you're leading your children. And your children are going to lead their children. You're leading a whole bunch of people, it's just that most of those people are not yet born. So, you are a black leader right now if you have kids, and if you don't have kids, you're going to one day be a leader when you do have kids or, anybody else who you influence. If you choose to be a leader, you're a black leader. So, I would argue that the best black leaders are people that can be proactive, and prepare.

And that's where insurance comes into play because insurance is a reflection of your desire to prepare for all the things that can go wrong. I spend the majority of my time talking about, or talking to my team, about insurance plans. Talking about estate planning, talking about what's in my will, talking about trusts, talking about stress tests, or what-if scenarios. What if we lose this revenue stream over here, what's going to happen to that? Are we prepared for that?

And so, with insurance, I encourage you to check your insurance. Make sure you have life insurance, for yourself and for your children. I know two children that died this year, and their parents were not prepared for the funeral, and it only made things worse. I know you don't want to think about having your children die, but life insurance for children doesn't cost anything. It's a few pennies, a couple dollars a month or whatever, and it gives you security in case something goes wrong. And it doesn't mean your kid is going to die, it just means you're prepared in case something goes wrong, and you don't have the emotional turmoil compounded with financial problems as well. Life insurance for yourself is necessary. If you care about your kids, you're going to get life insurance for yourself.

Health insurance is important. A lot of black people, especially black men, don't have health insurance. That only leads to more economic calamity, because one of the greatest pathways to lifelong debt is to get sick. You get sick, you're done. You can't pay those bills. Costs too much. And then, if you don't address the illness, then, yes, if it's something that's killing you, then it will kill you. Because you didn't go to the doctor.

Disability insurance is, in case you get injured, whether it's on the job or off the job, it makes sure that your income can maintain itself, so I encourage you to look into disability insurance. Get property insurance to protect your property. If you run a business, and if your business is anything like mine, then in the beginning, you're going to be one of the key components to that business. So, as one of the key components to that business, then you want to say, well what happens if I'm gone? What happens if I am unable to maintain this business? Or if I die or if I become ill? Insurance allows you to protect against that and to protect your assets. So, with my company, when we got to a certain level, I had extensive conversations about making sure that there would be some money available to my partners in case I wasn't here.

Estate planning, estate planning is critical. Let me tell you a secret about estate planning. Estate planning is what happens after you die. Let me tell you a big secret about estate planning that I heard from a lawyer. There's a lawyer who told me that the way her firm makes most of their money is from people who don't properly plan their estate. She said, "I hate it, but we make the bulk of our money because people live life as if they are never going to die." And then what happens is, everything they have goes into probate. When it goes into probate, then your kids aren't getting the money, the lawyers are getting the money. It becomes a big mess, it may destroy your family. You got relatives fighting in court, it becomes a complete fiasco. And when it's all said and done, your biggest beneficiary becomes Uncle Sam. The IRS becomes the biggest beneficiary that you have. So, proper estate planning is critical.

In theblackstockmarketprogram.com, I cover estate planning again. We had an estate planning attorney in before, that video is in with your course content, so log in at theblackstockmarketprogram.com and you can take a look at that. But I'm going to bring in some more estate planning experts, because I want you to really be able to take the time and do what you do in church. What I want you to do, I want you to think about the afterlife.

You're thinking about the pearly gates, you're thinking about salvation, life after, etc. Well I encourage you to think about the afterlife in a different way. I want you to think about the afterlife in a way where you get over yourself. Stop thinking about what's going to happen to you when you die, start thinking about the people that you're going to leave behind. Because I can't tell you what's going to happen when you go to heaven or when you die, I don't know what's going to happen to you. I'm just going to be honest with you. I'm not an un-religious person, I believe anything is possible. I just need a little, I need proof. I like all ideas, my father's a pastor and I listen to him, and I listen to other people too.

But I don't really know what happens when you die, because I've never died before. It's never happened. When I die, if I get a chance to come back and tell you what happened, then I'll do that. But I don't know what's going to happen to me in the afterlife, and you know what, I really don't care. Because what I do know is that in the afterlife, you're going to be gone, and your loved ones will still be here on Earth. And their time on Earth is going to be either heaven or hell, depending on how much time you spent planning for the possibility that you might not be here no more.

So, the question you must ask yourself is, are you prepared for the afterlife? That is where making a will comes into play. That is where life insurance comes into play. That is where estate planning comes into play. That is where spending time learning about trusts comes into play. And we cover all this in class. Again, you can log in, get your course materials, theblackstockmarketprogram.com. Get everything in there. But, I just will tell you that if you don't plan for your death, then what can happen is that, number one, your family's going to suffer because they won't have the resources they need, everything they need will be locked up in court. And then two, if you have accumulated something, it's going to disappear because 70% of all families lose all their wealth within one generation. The question is: How are you going to end up in that last 30% that don't.

Also, 90% of all wealthy families lose all their wealth within two generations. So, when I think about my wealth, and personally, I think, how am I going to make sure that I'm not in that 90%? How am I going to-- I'm not thinking about how much we can accumulate in 2017, I'm thinking, how do I make sure that we allow this wealth to grow so that it'll be around in the year 2117? How do I make sure that my great-great-great-great-great-great grandkids who are not yet born can benefit from all the hard work I put in to become Dr. Boyce Watkins? So, that's what I encourage you to think about. That's what matters, that's how wealth works.

The last type of insurance is what they call umbrella insurance. Umbrella insurance is kind of what they call insurance for your insurance. Now, one secret about insurance that you may not know is that your health and your life and all these other forms of insurance, a lot of them, have caps. Especially the health insurance. Health insurance has a cap where you will get covered up to a certain amount of money.

When you get your insurance plan, make sure you look to see what the max is that they'll pay. A lot of people don't think about it because you don't think you're ever going to hit that ceiling. But when you hit the ceiling, there's usually a reason. You've got some really horrible thing going on physically, and it ends up causing you to die.

I knew a kid in Illinois that I was advocating for because he was, well, he was like a lot of our boys. He was big into sports in high school. And the thing is, they love you when you're doing well, but they don't love you when you're not. And so, this kid was playing wide receiver, big strong kid. And he took a hit that went bad, and he got paralyzed at the age of 18. I mean, peak of his life.

It was the prime of his life. He got paralyzed from the waist down. I mean his life was practically over at the age of 18. Everybody's feeling bad, school goes to his mother and says, Mrs. Wilson, we love your son, and we're going to take care of him. We have an insurance policy in place; it'll take care of him for the rest of his life.

But what the mother did not know is that the school did not plan for him to live that long because paraplegics don't live that long after their injuries. They tend to die within four or five years because the inability to even move your neck is major. You can't even lift your head to eat; you can't do anything. So, anyway, the school underestimated the strength of black people. Black people, again, we're just so amazing that it's hard to take us down.

Instead of dying in three or four years like they planned, the kid lived another 31 years by the time I met him. So, he lives another 13 years, without being able to move his neck at all. And it was the saddest scene ever; his mother dedicated her whole life to sitting by his bedside and taking care of his every need.

I went to see them because I was advocating for them, and let me tell you why I was there. I was there because his 24-hour care ended up costing more than they thought. It cost $100,000 a year. His insurance policy had a cap to it, and he hit the ceiling. They sent his mother a little letter saying, *Mrs. Wilson, your insurance policy has reached its limit. We're going to cut your policy at a certain date.*

We advocated; we screamed; we hollered, and I tried to shame the school into making a move. They didn't do anything. And they let this black man die. They let him die, and his mother was devastated. She dedicated her whole life to taking care of him. And a lot of it was because they did not know that the insurance policy had a cap to it.

So, what I would say to you is be cautious when you buy insurance. Make sure you know what the cap is. Get umbrella insurance, especially if you have something to lose, because umbrella insurance doesn't just cover your insurance if it hits the cap, but it also protects you in the event of things like lawsuits because once you start making money and once you get financially secure, your life will change in a lot of ways that are good and bad.

When you get financial security, it feels better and you're happier that you're able to help people. But then also, you become a target. You become a target of people that want to borrow money, or beg for it. You become a target of people who want to steal it. You become a target of people who want to see you. Lawsuits can devastate everything, so umbrella insurance is the way to protect against the lawsuits.

This reminds me of a conversation that I once had with Darryl Bell, who I'm actually going to bring into class. You might know Darryl from "A Different World." He played Ron, Dwayne Wayne's best friend. Every time Darryl and I talk, we talk for hours. I just have so much respect for him. The first time Darryl and I talked, he was talking about a T.V. show, I forgot which one it was, and he said it really upset him because when the black kids on the show were fantasizing about what it meant to be rich, they showed images that were kind of ghetto-ized.

Driving in Bentleys, another one of the kids was throwing money up in the air, like they do at the strip clubs. Another one was, I don't know, buying Gucci and Louis and everything else. And he said, that really bothered me because that's not wealth, and that doesn't end well for our kids.

So, this is not what black wealth looks like, this is what is marketed to you by white people. And it's something that we should reject as black people, something that we should resist. Black wealth doesn't usually look like this. We think that the sports contract is going to lead to the get rich quick scheme. When I hear about an athlete going broke after he's made, say, a hundred million dollars, and thrown all his money away, I don't just get sad for the money he lost.

I get sad for the money that he could have had, that he should have had, that disappeared too. So, when you throw away money, you're not just throwing away the money that's in your hand, you're throwing away all the potential of that money. It's almost like if you hurt a woman who's pregnant, it's not just the woman, it's the baby. Well, your money is pregnant until you decide to get rid of it.

Like images in popular culture, the sports scenario is interesting in the sense that it can be beneficial to those who are able to get there, but the problem is that number one, black people and black men especially over-invest in professional sports, and it ends up benefiting white-owned institutions because we're giving our whole lives to making them rich. But it's to our detriment, because there's nothing more pathetic than a guy who thought he was going to get to the NBA who didn't actually make it, who didn't get any education along the way, who didn't have anything else in place, who didn't prepare himself for the possibility that he might not be the next Lebron James.

The NFL is a complete loss. The NFL is not a wealth-building tool for black men. The NFL is a poverty development tool for black men. Even if you get drafted, many of the NFL players I know, most of the ones I know, are not wealthy now. When they retire, most of them are broke. Most of them have brain damage. A lot of them have damage to their bodies from over-investing their bodies in this sport that does not show much mercy to your long-term physical health. That's why they die young.

In addition to the hits that you're taking, you're always on these anti-inflammatory drugs. It leads to drug addictions; it also destroys the body's ability to do natural things. Taking steroids, for example, hurts the body. I knew a guy who played for the Seahawks, and he was taking so many steroids that he had erectile dysfunction at the age of 26 or 27. I remember that it was his wife who told me the story, and I remember thinking, *what*? At 26 or 27, you are still young.

I just thought that was strange. And so, what happens is, you'll see guys who experience health issues at young ages. I knew another guy who was on dialysis at an early age because his kidneys had stopped working because he was taking so many drugs.

So, the NFL, in my opinion, is culpable. Some say, *mama don't let your babies grow up to be cowboys*; I say, *mama don't let your babies grow up to be NFL players* because I really don't think that's a good long-term investment. And that's even putting aside all of the other issues. A lot of the guys have the financial problems that come with child support because when you're the athlete and you got all the girls, you're also making all of the babies.

Additionally, you also have the issue with a lack of education. There's something about the sport that doesn't encourage black men to be educated. They're educated about sports, but not educated about anything else. These are just very bad life investments.

When you think about investing, the first thing you want to think about is not, how do I invest my money? You want to think about what-- the important stuff you're investing. The important stuff you're investing is not the money, it's your life! That's why the investment of marriage is huge. If you invest yourself and your life and your future in the wrong person that's far more financially devastating than buying a bad share of stock. You invest your life to try to become a professional athlete, to go to the NFL where they're giving a couple of hundred jobs, and there are 20,000 applicants? Are you serious right now?

So, think about your investments in a broad context, not just money. Investing goes far deeper than money. You're investing right now by being in this room. You could be doing a lot of stuff other than sitting here listening to me. You're listening to me because you're investing for your future, and you have some belief that this information I share with you is going to help you build a better life for yourself. And for that, I commend you. So, black wealth and wealth building doesn't usually look like that. It doesn't look like an NBA player, or a rapper. It tends to just look like this. And I like this image a lot, because it reflects the way I view the wealth building process.

Building wealth is a lot like building a building. When you build a building, you are going to go brick by brick. You are going to lay out the diagram of the building you want to build, and you are going to go piece by piece, brick by brick by brick, and it takes a long time. Wealth building is not get rich quick. It's something that happens slowly but surely. Financial security is something that will occur if you give yourself time to get there. You're not going to get it overnight.

So, money grows through time. Remember that wealth is an accumulation process. Just like growing a flower, etc. It's the tiny steps that matter. So, each day when you have some money, just sort of think a little bit more about what you're doing with that money. Think a little bit more about what you're doing with the more important asset, which is your time. When you have that time, I can tell you what, if you are thinking like a millionaire, and reading articles like a millionaire, and taking out The Wall Street Journal and reading the *CNN Financial* website, and reading books on business ownership, etc., it's going to change the DNA, the very fabric of the DNA, that makes you tick. It's going to change everything about how you see yourself, how you see the world, how you make your next move, what you do with your time.

I have lost my ability to be ignorant, to be honest with you. I can't sit around and waste time and do dumb things. Because I'm sitting here thinking about everything that's being lost by me wasting time doing what everybody else is doing. I'm always thinking about wealth building, I'm always thinking about investing, I'm always thinking about—not financial wealth building, I'm thinking about the community in terms of what we as a community can do. If we took everything we had and applied it toward building as opposed to applying it toward destruction, or giving it all away. The tiny steps are what matters.

You've already made somebody a millionaire, not just yourself. Remember that, if you've been paying rent for twenty years, you probably made your landlord a millionaire. In fact, I could probably do a math equation for you. Let me think here. Let's say that you put $1,000 a month into an apartment. Let's say you got an apartment where your rent is $1,000 a month. So, let's do the basic math. So, let's say you do $1,000 a month over the course of a year that's $12,000 a year, that's $120,000 over a ten-year period. Over thirty years, that's $360,000. That's pretty bad, right? Like, oh my god. $360,000 that I've given away. That's insane. In fact, the number seems so high that I want to double check the math here, let me make sure.

This is assuming your rent doesn't go up, which we know that it is, but I want you to keep the math very basic here. Here's where you really are going to get pissed off, when I tell you this. This is what's really going to hurt your feelings. That $360,000 is nothing. It's only the tip of the iceberg in terms of what you gave away. Remember, you didn't just give away the rent money. That's bad enough. What you gave away was your possibilities as well. You gave away opportunity as well. You gave away the fertility of that money. You didn't just give away what the money was, you gave away everything that money was born to become.

Understand this: if you pay rent for thirty years and you accumulate $360,000 that you've gifted to your landlord, because apparently, I guess you're just struggling so you can't build anything, but you've given away $360,000. That $360,000, had it been invested in the stock market-- let's say you've been doing it since the early '90s, or something like that-- that $360,000, had it been invested in the stock market in a diversified portfolio, earning a mediocre return consistent with the growth of the S&P 500, would have probably grown to about 3.5 million dollars. 3.5 million dollars, so you didn't just buy your landlord a house, you bought your landlord three mansions. That's what you did. You bought your landlord three mansions by paying rent to your landlord over that long period of time.

So, I'm not telling you what to do. I'm just telling you to get out. Get out of the rut of struggle-nomics, and get into the mindset of power-nomics. Now, I know buying real estate is not easy. I know that you have to make down payments and all of that stuff, but if you go over to theblackrealestateschool.com, you will find some helpful information that will help you get started. Andre Hatchett has a program called Real Estate 101.

Andre wanted to own a home, and Andre was making $15.15 an hour. $15.15 an hour. And he just sacrificed, he did something that is literally taboo, almost like a curse word in the black community. He made a sacrifice for his future, and he saved every penny, he kept track of his money for two or three years, because he basically said, I'm going to spend a couple years living like nobody else will, so I can spend the rest of my life living like nobody else can. That allowed him to buy his first home at the age of 22. He's been a homeowner ever since.

So, get off of this nonsense that, oh it's just too hard to own a home because I need a down payment. If you just take the time to educate yourself on how to buy real estate, you'll find that there are options out there that require very little money down. Some of us might be homeowners. Being a homeowner does not require you to be rich. It just requires you to not have a poor person's mindset, most of the time. It requires you to re-prioritize how you think about your money.

And I'm not criticizing; I'm just saying that maybe we should consider wealth building to be as important as getting our hair done. Or maybe wealth building should be as important to you as buying the new Jordans when they come out, or going out to the movies. That's it, I'm not asking you to change who you are. I'm just simply saying that you should just add something to your list of priorities. Make you and your future as important as instant gratification. That's it. That's it. Think about the future as much as you think about the present. And then you can get ahead.

Next, start the process today. You can do little things today. Maybe start by making a budget. Look at how much money you make, figure out what your expenses are, and then figure out where you can find a little bit of extra money to start saving right now. A lot of you in the stock market program, you already have apps like Acorns and Stash and Robinhood, to start investing. I love Acorns because you can put a few pennies in every couple of days, or whatever, and it can grow. I know a kid who works with me, who is 23, and he said, "I've been able to save up $400 in my Acorns app because I'm adding the extra change from my credit card."

So, I encourage you just to start small. And then also do the free stuff first, learning doesn't cost you very much. I mean, maybe if you're in one of our programs, yeah, it might cost you about the cost of going to the movies a couple times in a month. But for the most part, learning information doesn't cost you anything. When you're not here with me and learning from me, get on the internet. Read articles. Just consume information. And I'm going to leave you with this, and then I'll be done. And thank you for reading this. I'm really meditating on this issue and I want to make sure you internalize this and understand what I'm saying.

If you want to be a strong black person in America, you must be informed. If you want to be a strong black person in America, you must educate yourself. You must learn. I don't care if you're 12, or if you're 112. Being black in this country demands and requires and dictates that we are on the absolute cutting edge when it comes to competitiveness, when it comes to information, and when it comes to forward thinking and planning. If we get to the cutting edge of those areas, then we have the chance to not just assume equity in our own future, but we also have the ability to surge ahead. So, I'm not talking about equality or inclusion, I'm talking about dominance.

But really, it starts with your own family. Don't worry about saving the whole black community, you can leave that to people like me. I'm a public figure, I guess, so I'll lay out the big master plans and I'll ask you guys to help me if you trust me enough to help. But start with your own family. That's your own black community, and you control that. And I encourage you to just be a little bit audacious about it. Say, you know, in our family, we want to build wealth. We want to be like the Rockefellers, we want to be like whatever. Keep your values and your ethics intact, but at the same time, really have fun with the process. Because, I'll tell you, being empowered and being educated is a whole lot more fun than being a victim. It really is. I don't think this whole victimhood thing works for us, I think it makes us look silly, I think it makes us less than what we're supposed to be. I think that it makes us a fraction of what we're supposed to be as a community. And I don't think we're going to get anywhere with that.

I hope that after reading this chapter, you can identify with what financial security looks like. Tell people, go talk to your relatives about it. If we don't know, we can't grow.

CHAPTER 6

PROTECTING YOUR WEALTH

Building wealth and positioning yourself to think and execute like a millionaire requires work, sacrifice, and endurance. I think about this often when I think about what individuals like Dr. Claude Anderson and others have done for our people.

In a way, it's a lot like playing for a team, specifically, a basketball team that's going through a rough patch. It's like how they let the black coaches take over the college teams when they're losing the most. Or when Obama became president, they gave him the economy right when it was at the pits of hell. A lot of times our truest leaders, those who are really advocating for us, are the ones who are not only disrespected the most by America, but they're disrespected by their own people. They're disrespected by their own community because we know that the brainwashing is real deep. It's persistent because it has occurred over a very long period of time.

There was a study that said that it's going to take about nine generations for black people to catch up with other people, mainly white folks, when it comes to wealth. That generation is about 228 years. I thought about that study. Right? The more I thought about that, the more I concluded that that study is laced with just a little bit of bullshit. Let me tell you why. I hope I don't offend you. Every now and then a cuss word comes out. Blame my dad, because I can't apologize for it.

The reason why the study bothered me, is that, basically, it assumed that because you're behind in a race, if enough time passes you, you are going to catch up. Eventually, the gap will narrow and you're going to catch up. But that's a very, very, very bad assumption. That's assuming that you're running fast enough to catch up. That's assuming that your opponent is not out-running you. That's assuming that you're moving forward and not standing still. We got a whole lot of Negros that are running backward. They are running south when they're supposed to be running north.

My prediction is that if we don't win this battle in this generation and the next and the one after that, this battle for the souls of black people to get us to listen to information that makes sense, then in 228 years they're going to say, "Well, it's going to take another 500 years to close the gap." The gap will not close. The gap will widen because if you look at the studies across America in terms of how wealth is split up and spread out and controlled by certain people, you're not seeing the gap in wealth between rich folks and everybody else closing up. I'm not just talking about black. I'm talking about everybody. That gap is widening.

It's widening because, in the game of capitalism, there are those who understand it and those who do not. There's inheritance absolutely, but then there's a greater inheritance of information. I think that's the most important inheritance that there is. Even more so than wealth. Why do we say that?

Well, because there are studies that have also shown that most wealthy families lose all their wealth within one generation. 70% of wealthy families lose all their wealth in a generation. 90% lose all their wealth in two generations. The reason that they lose their wealth is because we think an economic inheritance is the most important variable. But if you don't inherit information, discipline, financial intelligence and a culture that breeds economic growth as opposed to struggle-nomics, then you're going to find that even a rich person's going to be broke by the time they're done.

When we look at these studies and we look at where we are and where we have to go, one of the reasons I want to encourage you is to help you remember that where you are right now means almost nothing relative to where you're going. We are only here for a blip in time. If you look at the history of great nations, and I've thought about this a lot because I want to see black people built into a great nation, if you look at how great nations are built one thing you understand is that this building process doesn't happen quickly. It doesn't happen in two or three years. It doesn't happen because you have one leader or it doesn't happen because you give a few good speeches. It happens, sometimes, over many, many generations, hundreds of years.

Be mindful that we're only here for a blip in time, but we're also participating in this long relay race called wealth building. It is not a solo race; it's a relay race and you are doing it right now all by yourself because your teammates aren't even born yet. We're handing off the baton in a few years when all of us are old, gray, and dead and gone. When you're running this relay race, we must understand that this is a race where our best shot, the most important thing that we can do in this generation, is not feel that we have to build every empire that's meant to be built. The most important thing that we can do in this generation is plant the seeds and let our children and grandchildren finish the job.

In fact, think about it like the way you watch a tree grow. A sycamore tree is the biggest tree that there is, one of the biggest that there is. If you look at the seed of a sycamore tree, it's very, very small. But if you want to grow a sycamore tree, you plant as many as you can and you give it time and you make sure the tree has plenty of sunlight, plenty of water, fertile soil and the ability to grow and with the passage of time you'll see the growth of that tree. Sycamore trees are not built in a day. Wealth is not built in a day. Most wealthy families are built over many, many generations of everybody playing on the same team, running the same relay race.

In fact, I could show you equations that define how money grows. All of the ways money and investment grows for any financial asset in the universe there are pretty much two or three equations that define the majority of how those assets grow. In those equations, the most important variable is time. Those equations are actually taken from biology because the way money grows is similar to the way a plant grows, the way a flower grows. My biggest concern for black folks is not where we're at. It's not that we don't have as much as we need to have or that we're going through a struggle right now. My biggest concern is that we're not planting enough seeds and we're not creating fertile soil for those that want to plant those seeds.

Let me give an example. How many of you all have families where if you come home and you tell them you got a new job, they want to pop bottles and throw a party? But then you tell them you're starting your own business, they act like it's a funeral. They feel sorry for you. "Well, the white man must not have wanted you. Well, just hang in there baby. One day we're going to get you that job." Right?

Then what they do is they subtly disrespect you. If you have a job now, they know how to define what you do. Your grandma be like, "Yeah, my baby he works over at Frito Lay. He puts the writing on the backs of the bags." And she's so proud because he's the vice president at Frito Lay and he's making $100,000 a year doing nothing, building a business, building an empire for somebody else.

But you're so proud because you see Frito Lay as this thing that's very real, that's real to you. It's almost as if you've been validated because our self-esteem is so affected that we need other people to validate us. We feel like we're worth nothing unless somebody comes along and tells us that we have value. When you do that people understand exactly what you do, but when you start a business, you see the same relatives and they're like, "What do you do again?" Or they act like you don't really have a job, "Since you aren't working can you go pick up the laundry and get the mail and go get the kids." They don't respect what you're doing. They don't understand the fundamental reality which is that every great empire that exists in America started as a figment of somebody's imagination.

In order for this building to be built, somebody had to imagine this center and draw up the diagrams to build the center and then go get the brick and mortar and everything else it took to develop this structure that we're in. In many ways those who are truly committed to building for the black community are kind of seen as a little bit crazy because much of the empire that you see, all the vision that you see right now, is a figment of your imagination. But I'm going to tell you that it's okay to be crazy. You need crazy people to build a nation.

I can tell you this, I don't know the answers to every problem that we have as a community. I don't pretend to be that person, nor will I ever be. But one thing that all of us can agree upon, I would imagine, is that what we've been doing is not working. What we've done to this point has not worked. Many of us are trained from birth to be part of an economic and social and political cage that is built for you before you're even born. A lot of us are like animals in captivity and we don't even know that we're born in the zoo. We really are the animal who lives in the zoo who really thinks he's free because he's never known what it means to be free.

People that I know when they get free, when they get off the corporate plantation, when they get out here, they really start doing things for black folks, they can't go backward. Animals understand freedom. You don't have to explain to an animal why it's better to be free than it is in a cage. Just let him out. You try to put him back in, he's not going to go back. But many of our people are born in a cage. Think about this. The first thing that we do is we hand our children over to oppressors, to people who hated them for 400 years, and say, "Here educate my baby." And then wonder why so many of our kids grow up screwed up. Think about that.

It takes about 187,000 hours to raise a baby from zero to the age of 18. During that 187,000 hours, they spend about 14,000 hours in school until they get to the age of 18. Some still can't read, write, or do math, but somehow, they have memorized the lyrics of every song that comes on the radio. They have *mastered nothingness*. They have mastered all of the things that are irrelevant to their development as a strong black person in this society. The brainwashing runs deep. You're being exposed to propaganda every day. You're being educated in a specific way every day, whether you turn on the radio, turn on the T.V., go to school or work for that corporation. Whatever it is, your thinking is being shaped.

The first thing that we have to do, as a people, if we're ever going to build anything is we have to reclaim the education of our children in every single way. Let me tell you this, when I'm talking to the people in this room and I'm looking in your eyes, what I'm really seeing are people that are kind of like, what they call, preaching to the choir. I don't think you would be here if you were lost. I don't think you would even be here if you were a person who needed to hear this information. And what I really believe is most of the black economic revolution is going to be led by people who I call the early adapters.

The early adapters are the people who are kind of like economic soldiers. You think about the military. You don't need everybody to be a soldier. You just need a few good men and women so my argument is that we, as the economic soldiers, we as the choir, we as the people that are taking the lead on this, have a mandate to make sure that as we raise our children we teach them to develop business, to develop structure, to really get the most out of their talents.

We have to kill the old paradigm of what is considered to be black success which is go to school, work hard, and get a job, and give 40 years to that job and then you die at your desk and then you disappear and they replace you within a week and act like you were never there. That's not success. Somebody told you it was success. For many of you there was a point where you started thinking about it, you say, "Wait a minute. I think I'm successful. I was told I'm successful, but I don't feel successful." That's because you're not. You were told you were free, but you're really aren't free. You had to kind of figure it all out as you went along.

I would argue that what we can do for our children is make sure they don't have to go through that process. They're hearing this from birth, from the very beginning, for example, point blank, period. No black child in America should be raised under the assumption that you're going to grow up and work for somebody else. From the minute your child learns how to say, "Mama, can I have some money?" You don't say, "Well, boy, one day you got to grow up and get you a job." No, you say, "One day you're going to grow up and start you a business." That's what you do. Now if they want to figure out how to go work for other people as part of their plan, that's fine. But that should be Plan B. That should never be Plan A.

Additionally, I believe that black people can be successful. We can do whatever we want without changing a thing about who we are. We're already extraordinary people. Let's be real. We are the descendants of the survivors of the Middle Passage. We are the descendants of the survivors of the worst slavery and the worst atrocities in all of human history. They really can't kill us. The only people that can really kill black folks are other black people. That's why they train you to turn the gun on yourself. You saw hip hop as a tool for empowerment, so they flip it over and say let's use it as a tool to kill black people.

The fact is that they can't kill us. They can't take us down. Who we are is fine. It doesn't require an overhaul in terms of how we conduct ourselves. It simply requires modest tweaking. For example, I don't believe that it makes any sense whatsoever for a black boy to spend more time on the football field then he spends in a book or in the classroom or learning how to start a business. Black men are the most unemployed group of people in America and the foundation, the core, the crux, the reason that your families are falling apart and the reason the black women don't respect you anymore is because you're out here, as a man, begging another man to feed your children. If I know that I'm the reason, if I'm the white man, I know that I'm the reason that your children get to eat every day, you're not the man of your house, I'm the man of your house.

We must help black boys understand that there ain't nothing out there for them. There ain't no opportunities waiting for you, black man, especially if you went to prison. It's a lie. It's a false dream. It's some hocus sprinkled in front of you to get you to behave just long enough to let your guard down so they can slaughter you. If you don't believe me, look around and see how many black men you see committing suicide on a daily basis. I'm not talking about killing themselves, some of them actually kill themselves. I know a lot of former athletes who gave everything trying to get into the NFL then found out at the last minute there aren't that many jobs. I know a lot of guys like that who've actually killed themselves.

I'm not talking about the guys who killed themselves blatantly or literally. I'm talking about the guys who kill themselves slowly over time. Like the guy sitting at home every day, smoking weed, getting drunk every day, in his drawers playing X Box in his mama's basement because a white man won't give him a job because he somehow has been led to believe that his free time, his 40 hours a week, that the white man might pay for, has no value if white people have not acknowledged that value.

Think about that. Why would he pay you to come to work 40 hours a week if your labor did not have value? So, therefore, if he's not paying you for that labor, why are you not able to take that labor and apply it to something of your own and extract that value for yourself? If he's paying you $20 an hour, that probably means you're worth $70 an hour. Why aren't you equipped to take that labor and apply it to something that's going to benefit your family directly as opposed to benefiting somebody else?

A lot of it is because when you were a kid, you spent more time learning how to be a basketball player, football player, and a rapper then you spent learning how to be a man.

This is warfare, people. This is warfare. That which makes a man marriable, in many cases has to do with his ability to provide for himself and provide for other people. That which gives the man pride is connected to his ability to provide. I can tell you I became deeply offended as I grew up and moved into manhood and started to realize, "Wait a minute. Hold on. Wait. In order for me to feel like a man, I have to go beg this other man to take care of me like I'm a baby. I don't feel like a man right now. I feel like a little boy. I'm feeling kind of like a bitch right now."

What I'm saying to you is that the very basis of the assumptions that we make about what it means to succeed in this society have to go out the window. About 70 or 80% of the so-called successful black people we see every day really aren't successful. They aren't successful. They are individuals who have been given financial rewards for bowing down and supporting white supremacist institutions. If you know anything about white supremacy, if you know anything about capitalism, you understand systems reward you for supporting the system.

If you reject the system or question the system or challenge the system, the system's designed to spit you out. In many cases, the successful black person is not the one who got to the top of the pile. A lot of times, it's the person who got booted out, but because we are so trained to think in a specific way about what black success really means, because we've been taught to mistake success of assimilation, we will often celebrate the least successful people in our community.

One good example, mind you, is right here in L.A., the guy named Lee Daniels who makes that stupid show *Empire*. He humiliates our community by making all of these movies that are incredibly disrespectful to black people, but many black people consider him to be a role model or consider him to be a successful man because some white guy wrote him a check. We need to get off of that. We need to let that go right now and challenge those people for that kind of behavior.

Let me say this to you. Let's get into some specifics on some strategies that we can apply in order to do what we have to do. Now one of the people that I love the most and respect the most is Dr. Mulligan. Dr. Mulligan often mentions Dr. Claude Anderson. Dr. Anderson wrote a book, a lot of books, but one of the books I consider to be one of the greatest books ever written in the history of this world is *Black Labor White Wealth*. Another one would be *Powernomics*. One of the things that Dr. Anderson talks about, specifically, that I think we want to really focus on, and meditate on, is the fact that we need leadership that has a plan.

The problem is that we have too many leaders who will hoot and holler and complain and get everybody riled up and then nothing happens afterward. There's no structured, systematic, step by step, day to day process that we can all follow that will help us achieve the empowerment that we're looking for. The other thing that we have to just accept right now, at least in this generation, is that we're not the popular kids on the block. There'll never be a day where we're speaking about this stuff, not in our lifetime, where this room is as full as it would be if there was a Beyoncé concert or something like that.

My argument would be that as we move forward, rather than always feeling like we have to carry the burden of saving an entire community and carrying all that on our backs, we can do what we need to do individually within our sphere of influence to develop economic strength and security in our own families. People often talk about building the next black wall street. How do you build the new Black Wall Street?

A lot of times what they visualize is something that's tough to accomplish. They're visualizing something that's worth hundreds of millions of dollars and consists of a lot of buildings and shops and everything else all up and down the block. This will exist over time, but if you study how economies work, you realize that an economy can be giant or it can be small, but the dynamics can be very much the same. A black wall street does not have to be brick and mortar buildings. A black wall street can also be digital.

I look at technology and I see what's happening on the internet where black people come together to form digital villages and talking to each other every day. It's really powerful and transformative. Most black people who know anything about me now would never know about me were it not for technology because they're not going to let a negro like me on T.V. That isn't going to happen. We know that. If I had a show, I'd lose that show in about a week. Right? Technology is one of the avenues of possibility that exists for us.

Also, it is an avenue for wealth building in terms of the ability for us to do business with each other and, actually, you may not know this but 80% of the wealth generated on this planet has been generated, in the last two years, in Silicon Valley. Our children are aiming for the wrong dreams. I would argue that if we generate children who are masters of technology and entrepreneurship then those individuals will create the next Snapchat. They will create the next Facebook. They will create whatever.

But what we have to do as a community, as well, is we have to create fertile soil for black entrepreneurs so that those businesses can grow because, imagine this. Imagine you have a kid and he's really good with computers and he's as smart as Mark Zuckerberg who created Facebook and he says, "You know, I'm really good at computers. I have this great idea. Here's what I'm going to do." Is he really going to get support from every black person he sees to say, "You know, you can create a billion-dollar company." Or is somebody going to say, "You know, Pookie, you're good with computers. They will pay you $200,000 a year to go work at IBM." That's what they do. That's what I was told. That's what people like me were told.

We have to have fertile soil. We also have to understand how economies work and what that really means. One of the things that I can share with you is a model that, I believe, in a very basic, simple way allows you to ensure that any child that is in your sphere of influence, your children, your grandchildren, anybody else, will have a very high probability of becoming a millionaire between the ages of 30 and 40. The model's very basic. It's the word KID. K-I-D. I came up with this model just for black people.

It's very easy to implement.

The 'K' stands for knowledge. 'I' stands for investment. 'D' stands for discipline. Knowledge. Investment. Discipline. KID. What does the knowledge part mean? Well, the knowledge means that your child's understanding of financial literacy and wealth building should start at an early age. It should be as fundamental as our commitment to sports and entertainment. It should be as fundamental as going to church every Sunday. If you ask a kid who grew up in a church, "When's the first time your grandma took you to church?" They won't remember. I would argue that we should have children where they can't remember the first time their parents taught them about economic intelligence or how to start a business. It should be a part of the culture.

They should also have some degree of financial literacy training at an early age. Every black child in America should know how to start their own business by the age of 12. Just as a rite of passage. As fundamental as their responsibility. We had something in Los Angeles about two months ago and there was a mother who came in. She showed me a video of her four-year-old twin sons and they had memorized impressive information. We had given them a little curriculum and they were able to demonstrate what they learned. She showed me a video of her four-year-old sons reciting the curriculum. She said, "Sometimes it's hard because the other parents think I'm too serious because I don't let my kids watch T.V.; I don't let them eat garbage like McDonald's, or stuff like that. I make sure they're learning financial literacy and not Nicki Minaj lyrics." I said, "You know what? You're the key to all of this."

The mother's the key to everything. The mother is the first master teacher and then the father comes in second. We know we can't do this without the mothers getting on board with these ideas. I said, "What you've basically done is you have guaranteed that your sons will never be unemployed." A person who knows how to think entrepreneurially from a fundamental sub-conscious level is a person who's able to see opportunity everywhere.

They can walk into a room where there's no money and see wealth everywhere. It's like the difference between somebody who knows how to just hunt for a job versus somebody who knows how to start their own business. It's like the difference between somebody who only feels like they can eat when the restaurants are open versus somebody who knows how to grow their own food, hunt their own food, cook their own food. Who's going to eat better? Who's got more food security? The person who only knows how to go to McDonald's and Burger King or the person who knows how to grow and cook their own food?

A lot of us were raised in wonderful families where consciousness was taught to us at an early age. I wasn't in that family. I was raised in a very typical, stereotypical family, where I was taught a lot of the wrong things. I picked up these ideas in my 30s so I didn't have the advantage that our children can have because it took a long time for me to un-program myself from all the other crap I had learned and re-program myself into something that was actually going to help me succeed in this country. Did you know that if they took every super computer on the planet and put them all together, they still cannot simulate one human brain? You literally are walking around with a super computer on your hands and the most powerful part of that super computer is the part that you don't even see. It's the sub-conscious mind.

The messages that you get at an early age shape you in ways that you can't even imagine. My argument, my belief is that with our children we hit the sub-conscious early, we hit it hard, we hit it consistently with messages of empowerment, economic intelligence and all the things that they're going to need in order to be successful because the thing you've got to understand is that economics is not a nice game to play. It's warfare. Global economic warfare is what runs this country. Economic protectionism is what occurs in every single community.

Unfortunately, many of us did not get the memo. When you drop your child in the middle of an economic system and they've never been trained in economics, that's like dropping them in the middle of the Super Bowl and they've never seen a football. They've never had football practice. They don't know which end zone is theirs. They don't know how to score points. You put that child in that situation, they are going to get killed.

What's going to happen to that child? You drop them in the middle of the Super Bowl and you're not prepared to play. You don't know what to do. You don't have any shoulder pads. You don't even know what a football looks like. You don't know the difference between the referee and the cheerleaders versus the people in the stands.

Well, you're going to end up having to serve a master who will offer to protect you or you're going to walk up to your opponent and say, "Can you explain the rules of this game to me?" They'll say, "Sure. The first thing you've got to do is every time you get the ball, you're supposed to give it to me. Don't worry about scoring your own points. I'll score all the points and I'll give you some points." And then you wonder why every game ends with you losing 187 to 2. But that's what we do when we send our children out into the economic system, a competitive global economic system, without economic training.

We are putting them in the middle of a battlefield without a gun, without a shield, without a strategy, without training, without nothing. When you're in that situation, all you can do is serve people who offer to protect you and you will end up learning the rules of that battlefield from the people who are going to oppress you in exchange for that information or in exchange for that protection. The information that they give you is going to be false. That's what we're doing when we're learning how to play the game of economics from the people who hate us the most, who live off of our exploitation.

You see, capitalism benefits from that. Let me paint yet another picture. Do you want to consume for the rest of your life or do you want to own? Do you want to be the employee or the employer? Do you want to be the landlord or the renter?

My purpose in asking these questions is not to make you feel guilty about some of your choices; instead, it is to help you see the spectrum of choices that we often make as it relates to wealth.

CHAPTER 7

IT'S NOT TOO LATE: BEING A MILLIONAIRE BY RETIREMENT

The first thing I want you to understand as we talk about this, is that I'm not just talking about you. You see, a lot of people talk about becoming a millionaire as something that happens because you got lucky. They say, you joined the right MLM, or you did day trading and you made the right trade. I don't teach Day Trading, not because there aren't people who make money at it, but because, it's a rollercoaster. If I see a hundred of you all go Day Trade, half of you are going to make some kind of money and the other half are going to lose money. A couple of you are going to make a lot of money, and a few of you are going to lose a ton.

I can't ethically send you off to Day Trade; you can learn that from a different person. Day Trading is a reflection of every nightmare that your grandma had about the Stock Market, and how scary the Stock Market is, because that's where you see the fluctuations, the ups and downs, the crazy stuff.

In fact, Day Trading is a lot like moving to a new city. There are some parts of the city you can live that are nice and safe, and there are some places that are like the "Hood." Some places represent the dark allies. I'm not going to send you down the dark allies of investing because I can't take responsibility for what's going to happen, if you walk down those dark allies.

I'm leading everyone to the nice comfortable, safe suburbs, just in this case, the suburbs happen to be black. With that being said, what I want to talk about is systematic, structured ways to become millionaires by the time you're 65.

Some of us believe that this is not doable. Some of us do not know millionaires in real life, so we cannot see ourselves as millionaires. If you reflect back to Chapters one and two, remember that we have to shift our mindsets in order to begin true wealth building.

Let me ask you a question: How old are you *right now* as you are reading this?

What if I told you that about 80% of what you've been taught all of your life is nonsense. Most of us are still young enough to change a lot of things, maybe you're reading this book because you're ready to consider transitions, either in your day to day choices, or in your overall career.

I had a meeting with a woman not too long ago, who was a business associate, and she's about 32 or 33, and she said, "You know, I used to just really think that a lot of the stuff you did was too much and too radical." She was very political; she was the Democratic Representative for her section of the city, and was kind of hobnobbing with a lot of elite people, and trying to get in those circles, and she said, "I started realizing that racism is everywhere, and I just hate it." And I said "Yeah, I know it's everywhere." She said, "I just decided to start being myself." And I said, "Well, you know, you were amazing before white people started to acknowledge you. You do know that right?"

Too often, I'm seeing people in their thirties having these "wake-up moments" where they are climbing out of everything that they might have been taught—not to the point where they're walking away completely from what they were before, but to the point that they're enhancing who they are in order to become who they were intended to be. In other words, they are circling back into their true strength.

And that is what I want to encourage you to keep doing; keep circling back into your strength because you're never going to be best if you're imitating somebody else. The original is always going to be better than the substitute. Don't be the substitute; instead, be yourself.

But here's the thing, I don't care if you're 114 years old and you're reading this—there's a reason that you're here, and it really goes to the core of why you invest in the first place— keep learning.

You're not investing just so you can die with a whole bunch of money. You're investing so that your family can build a legacy of wealth, an endowment that's going to last long after you're gone.

That's why an investor is supposed to think about the future. If you want to be a thorough investor, you want to think of your family as an ongoing concern. You have to get over yourself. You have to stop thinking about me, and mine, and what I'm going to have by a certain time. Stop asking: "How fast can I get money, Dr. Boyce?"

You can do that, but I'm telling you that when you learn this, and when you start making these moves and positioning things, what happens is you're passing things down to your children that give them the chance to take it to the next level. So, even if you're 87 or 97 years old and you're reading this, your job is to really start setting a trend and a pattern that will help you escape the economic and psychological traps that hurt the community.

It's very important that I start with that because, if you don't know why you're doing this then it's going to be hard to understand why you even want to make the sacrifice.

A lot of people don't invest, not because they don't have the money, not always because they don't know how, it's because they have no incentive. They have not fully internalized the why. And the why has to be greater than you, for you to really be committed to it. If you're just doing it for yourself, it's very difficult for you to really dig into this.

And also, if you're younger than 25, it is important that you start making changes now. I've told this to a 12-year-old who was asking me how to invest not too long ago. I was explaining to her about stash, and acorns and all of that because, I don't care how young you are, if you're ready, you need to start moving forward. The younger the better. I told her, "One day, you're going to have kids," and I said, "Your kids are going to be born; you're 12 and you may have kids in the next 15 years, or maybe 20 years, who knows. Your kids are going to need resources. You should start investing today for unborn children."

So, the same thing is true with grandparents you have unborn great grandchildren or great-great grandchildren. Start investing for them now. That's what I'm doing, I'm thinking about kids that don't exist yet. So that I can make sure that when they finally get here to this place called earth, that they are ready, to live well in the afterlife, and I'm talking about my afterlife. When I'm not here, after my life is over, I want to make sure that those people are living well.

So, how do you become a millionaire by retirement?

Okay, so, these are the rules and you can really call these the Dr. Boyce rules, only because, what I tend to do is, I don't take theories as they are. I enhance them based on what I've seen, what I know and what I know about being black and the unique challenges that come with being black. Nothing that you read here is something that you're going to see in *Rich Dad Poor Dad* or something written by Dave Ramsay or someone like that.

Because, I think that for black people, there's a uniqueness in terms of why we're doing this, we're trying to overcome oppression. Similar, not entirely similar, but somewhat similar to what the Jews were dealing with when they left Russia to create Hollywood. Also, we're dealing with limitations in terms of capital, challenges with family, dealing with the trauma from slavery, 400 years of slavery and oppression, the list goes on and on and on.

So, here's some basic rules that I want you to kind of keep in mind when it comes to figuring out how to become a millionaire by retirement.

I want you to think about sort of hitting that finish line, as something that is an accumulation of a series of thousands and thousands of very tiny efforts that you will repeatedly take over the course of time. And that's how people become wealthy. That's how people die millionaires.

Rule number 1: You want to invest early, and you want to invest often. Let's imagine a chart that shows the difference in wealth accumulation between people who've invested at the age of 25, versus 35, versus 45, versus 55.

Now, each of these people have pretty much put up $5000 a year in their investment portfolio. If you break $5000 a year down then that's a little bit more than $400 or $500 a month, maybe $400 to $425 a month, that's about the cost of a car note.

Look at the 25-year-old. The 25-year-old, let's call him investor A, starts off early, and he's ahead in the race before anybody gets started. And the interesting thing is that nobody is able to catch up with him because the 25-year-old, by the time he hits the age of 45 and 50, is making money on top of money, on top of money.

By the time he hits 50, before the 55-year-old even gets started, or around when the 45-year-old began, he's already got a quarter of a million dollars in a capital base. You see, you ever hear people say, "It takes money to make money?" Well, it doesn't take money to make money all the time, but having money makes it much easier to make more money. The more money you have, the more money you're going to make.

There are different kinds of people in this country. There are people who have no money, who can't find two nickels to rub together, and there are people who their number one problem is "I have too much money and I don't know where to put it."

Think about this, who buys a Treasury Bill from the Federal Government where the interest rate is like 0.1 and 0.2%? Or almost 0%? Who would buy an investment where the investment rate is so low, that it almost doesn't even exist? Well, the people who buy those assets, are people who have so much wealth, that they don't know what to do with their money. They're literally looking for places to put their money. By the time the 45-year-old gets started, the 25-year-old has accumulated a $200,000 head start. So, the 25-year-old is not only starting at a better place, but the rate of growth of his wealth is much higher than the 45-year-old because the 45-year-old is starting with a tiny base of nothingness.

My God, you can analyze universities, for example, to see what this looks like from an analogous standpoint. Harvard University has an endowment of like 36 billion dollars. Now if you look at their annual rate of return, I think they're able to generate over 10% a year of 3.6 billion dollars a year which would be about 300 million dollars a month, is that right? Am I doing the math right? Yeah, 300 million a month is about 10 million dollars a day. Think about that number—10 million dollars a day. And that's all because they have a capital base. Why should this matter to you?

What you want for your family is to think about the future. You need to go to your relatives and say, "People, what we need is a capital base." A capital base is something that allows you to keep making money even when you are asleep. Now capital base is not just financial assets, it's not just liquid money, it's not just a bunch of cash, or a bunch of treasury bills, or a bunch of stocks and bonds. No, a capital base is anything in place, that allows you to generate the resources that you need. A capital base could be a family business. A capital base if you're a farmer, could be a cow. You can get milk off that cow every day, or an apple tree can be a capital base. We don't get any money off the apple tree, but it's our tree and it keeps generating apples which therefore allows us to eat.

Anything that you have in place that allow you to keep getting the resources you need, that you can live off of, is a capital base. The reason black families struggle economically is because we have no capital base. What happens is we are going to other communities to get capital that we need in order to survive or get resources we need, because we're eating apples off somebody else's tree.

But nobody's telling black folks to go and plant apple trees. Instead, everyone's thinking how am I going to get an apple today so I don't starve to death, but somebody has to say, let's plant some trees, so our children are solving a different problem. Their problem is not how do we get apples to eat, their problem becomes we got so many dang apple trees, what are we going to do with these apples. That's what you want.

This 25-year-old, by starting his investing early, has gotten so far ahead, that they're never going to catch up with him. Not only is he far ahead, but his rate of growth is much higher. Remember I was telling you guys about financial fertility? If you haven't seen the lecture for financial fertility, go log in at theblackstockmarket.com. If you log in, you'll see the lecture where we talk about financial fertility and I talk about rabbits, and how giving birth to additional rabbits, you have more rabbits in each generation based on the number of rabbits that you had in the previous generation.

The amount of money that you have at a certain time dictates how much wealth you generate in the next segment of time or in the next cycle. Imagine this, the 35-year-old says, "Okay, that's all right, I can wait 10 years, it's no big deal." See all of you young people need to pay attention now.

You're thinking it's no big deal, I'll start at 35, well think about this, when he starts at 35, he's never going to catch up to the 25-year-old first and foremost. The gap at retirement is massive, $787,000 vs $364,000. He's $400,000 ahead of you. And if you're really crazy, I won't say crazy, but, if you start at 45, the 25-year-old is $600,000 ahead of you. If you start at 55, you're investor D. At this point, investor A is $700,000 ahead of you. Which investor is positioned to be more financially secure in this scenario?

So, you might think, *Oh, it's no big deal, I'll be making more money then, I can just put more money in here.* Do you not understand that investor B and investor C and D could double their investments and still be left behind? Yes, you read that correctly. I said double their monthly contributions and they still won't catch up to the 25-year-old.

The 25-year-old will win the race because he has the asset of time.

You know what it reminds me of? It reminds me of when I used to run track. I don't know if anybody else ran track, but I used to run this race. It was a horrible race called the 400-meter dash where you run one lap around the track. For whatever reason, it was the hardest race that there is because your body is so oxygen deprived and by the time you get to the finish line, your legs feel like they weigh a thousand pounds, you're about to pass out. I used to run this horrible race, it was like torture. What we used to think is that, in order to avoid the pain of running the race, I mean, the race was so painful, you'd literally throw up sometimes after you got done. That's how bad it was.

We thought that in order to avoid the pain, of the race, we would simply just chill out in the first half of the race, just jog the first half, and let everybody get a little bit of a lead, and then sprint and try to catch up. And my coach would say, "Boys, that's not going to work, because by the time you get done jogging, and you start running, they're going to be so far ahead of you, that it won't matter if they're tired, you still won't catch them."

I didn't listen to my coach, so I did it anyway. I jogged, I just kind of pranced about for the first 2-300 meters, and then I said, okay, now I'm feeling good, now I'm going to kick it in. By the time I decided to pick it up, they were so far ahead of me that I couldn't catch them.

Investing is the same way. The person who gets out the gate, who's consistent, gets so far ahead of everybody else. Here's a little secret about this chart they're not showing you, and this is what I'm adding in, because, I don't know why more people don't talk about this. The youngest person in this chart is 25 years old. Well what if he was 15? What if he was five? He might need some help at the age of five because five-year-olds don't make $400 a month. But their parents do.

If you start investing at the age of 5 that $780,000 for the 25-year-old grows into the millions. It's very easy, and this is only an 11% return, that's about the average return of the stock market over the last hundred years. It's really easy to turn a child into a millionaire because children are already millionaires. Remember, they have the gift of time. What's really hard is to turn 55 year olds into millionaires by the time they're 65 because they've let so much time go to waste. It's quite difficult.

Rule number 2: You have to be very consistent. The number one factor that kills all people's ability to accumulate assets is the inability to remain consistent. You want money to be automatically withdrawn from your account. You want to set it and forget it. You want to make it into a habit. You want your investment to be as consistent as eating.

Imagine if I took all the money that you spent going to McDonald's or going to Burger King over the years. You've done that very consistently if you eat fast food. Or maybe you don't like those places but you've probably gone somewhere, right? If I were to take all that up, and show you what you've made in the stock market, it would probably make you cry, and the interesting thing about it is that, that consistency is replicated in many sectors of our own lives. There's many things that you've done thousands of times, you've never thought about it. I mean, imagine if I made you count the number of times you've had sex in your life. I don't know, if you're lucky, I assume you're at least in the hundreds, some of you all are in the thousands, whatever, but I'm not judging.

Imagine if you added that up, you probably can't even remember all the times you've had sex. You can't remember all the times you've sat down for a meal. You can't remember all the times you got up and clocked in and went to work every day. You've done it thousands of times. But you don't remember. So, investing must be part of your consistency that makes up this thing called life for you.

Imagine if I asked the moms to count the number of hours that she spent talking to her children and raising her kids. That's something she's done very consistently because it's very natural. As such, investing should be the same way.

A person who is a consistent investor will never be broke. They just won't. Because they're going to have a consistent accumulation of capital. If the money is put to work, the money is going to make more money, even when they're doing something else, and you give that person 20 or 30 years, they're going to be absolutely fine financially, and in many cases, they're going to be worth over a million dollars.

The key is to be very consistent with whatever you do; just make it a healthy habit and stay with it.

Rule number 3: Increase your income base through entrepreneurship. Now one of the things that I'm going to show you this chart in a second, that's going to show you, precisely the amount of money that you'd have to invest in a diversified portfolio, remember from the very beginning we've always talked about diversification. When you invest in the stock market, rule number 1 is diversification.

If you haven't seen the lecture on diversification, go log in at theblackstockmarketprogram.com and watch lectures 1,2,3,4,5,6,7,8,9,10 where we talk about diversification and what that looks like.

When you're investing in a diversified portfolio, I'll show you exactly how much you have to put in every month to make yourself a millionaire by the age of 65 based on your age. Here's the interesting thing I've observed. Most people talk about your income as if it's static. They talk about what you can do with what you've got and how you can cut costs.

Well, I'll tell you why I broke that trend in my own life, because, I didn't want to cut my costs. I didn't want to live on a frugal budget. I didn't want to not enjoy my life as much as I did before. I said, "There has to be another solution."

The mathematics was very basic. Maybe instead of cutting the amount of money I spend, I can increase the amount of money that I make. That's where entrepreneurship comes into play.

There are very few communities where there are more entrepreneurial opportunities than in Black America. The reason is that because the community is so undercapitalized, there aren't that many businesses and there aren't that many businesses that actually get to grow. Also, the community culture is not one that's built on entrepreneurship. When you turn your children into entrepreneurs, they literally become instant power brokers in the black community because they'll never run out of black people looking for jobs.

I share this information far and wide, I go to all these cities and talk to a lot of people, but there are more people who don't listen to me than there are that do listen to me. Right? Maybe let's say that there's a couple million people who listen to me, well, there's about 38 million people who don't. And those people unfortunately are still looking for jobs.

When you make entrepreneurship part of your family culture, what you've done is directly increased your capital base in two ways. One, you've decided to work together. When you come together, that is an automatic increase in wealth. When you're working together, you're taking your energy and turning it inward instead of distributing your best energy, and your best expertise outward.

Instead of going out and working for white folks and doing things for them, you're doing things for your own family, and you're putting that energy toward your investment projects that relate to people that you love. You see, no matter what you're investing your time into, it can always go bad. If you go work at Target, or Walmart, that company could still fold. You could still lose that job. If you go and put the energy into your family business, yes, that business could fold as well, but at least, if it succeeds, the rewards are higher.

You see, investment is almost never a certain kind of thing. Investment is always a risk. I don't care how much of an expert you are at business, when you put your time and energy and your money into a business, there's always a chance it's not going to work out. Therefore, what you want to avoid is a mindset where you can only make an investment if you know for sure that it's going to work out.

I hate to tell you this, but there are not any certainties in this world. Nothing is certain. You might marry the man of your dreams, or the woman of your dreams, and it still might not work out. You just have to sort of make sure you're always ready with a plan B in case it doesn't work out.

I encourage you to increase your wealth by pouring your best energy back into your family. The other way you're increasing your capital base is through knowledge and information. So, if you're reading this, I encourage you to share what you have learned with friends and family or encourage them to buy a copy of the book. If you do that then what happens is that you share this information as well as other information. You're reading articles. You're reading books. You're having conversations. So, when you have people that come together and then they become smart people who are coming together, then wealth will come out of that.

You can't put a bunch of really smart people in a room together, who are all motivated to do something special, and not have something amazing come out of that.

Create a brain trust, within your family, and what this brain trust will do is it will give you a chance to increase your income base. And I will tell you what. As a man, who knows what it's like to be a millionaire, I'm not bragging, but I've been a millionaire for a little bit. I was a millionaire on paper a few years ago, and then the money eventually comes with it. I'm not bragging about that at all, but I have to tell you that so that you know I'm not just talking from theory. I'm talking from experience.

I will tell you, it's a lot easier to make financial moves when you can move thousands of dollars around whenever you want to. It's a lot easier to make financial moves as well, when you've got some money and you've got a crew of people who trust and love each other and really want to do well and you've got some knowledge in there. Knowledge and creativity.

When I get together with my brain trust of people that I work with, million dollar ideas fly off of the table. And not only do we have the ideas, and the trust necessary to execute those ideas, in our own little economy, we've also got the resources to make that move, because we've got our own bank. We stacked up our capital base, so that we don't need to go and say, "Well I hope Bank of America will give us this loan." because they're not going to do it.

We don't need to go out and say "I hope white America will support this initiative." Because, they're not going to do it. We can go back to our own capital base and make things happen. It's much easier to get to where you want to get to, if you're thinking entrepreneurially because then you are also thinking in terms of multiple streams of income, if there's someone in the family that loses a job, it's not a sad thing. If a skilled person loses their job, it should never be a sad thing. You should never be sad because someone who has talent and education doesn't have a job. That's a resource that's available for the family, that if it's properly applied, can be utilized to develop the capital base for your family.

When I hear relatives that have lost their jobs, if I have space in my organization, I'm like hey, let's get on the phone and let's figure out how I can justify what it's going to take for me to put some money in your pocket, and for you to help us build up this family business.

That's the thinking you want to have. You don't want to keep pushing the fish back into the water and just hope that somebody just picks them up, and if they don't pick them up then they must be worthless. That's not true. You're worth something, whether or not someone pays you for your time.

Rule number four: If you have a job and you have a 401k plan, max it out. Max it out. Especially if your company is putting in matching funds. I don't know if I've mentioned this to you guys, but I got so angry last week. I was watching SNL, Saturday Night Live, and they had this segment called Black Jeopardy, did I mention it? If I mentioned it last week forgive me for repeating myself but it made me so mad, I get to say it twice. They were basing it all on those stereotypes. One of the questions was, you know, on Jeopardy, they give the answer first then the question? And the host said, "The next answer is, your boss says they want to take $40 out of your paycheck for your 401k" and she answers the question, she says "Alex, what is, you better give me my $40 so I can buy me some scratch-offs." I couldn't believe it, it made me so mad. I'm sure there's a lot of black people that thought it's the funniest thing in the world, because they're like "yeah, you know how black people are, we don't invest, we want the scratch-off."

Well guess what, the scratch-off, would knock you off economically and leave you destitute when you don't have somebody else paying your bills anymore. The scratch-offs are what will lead you into poverty because a lottery ticket is literally one of the worst investments you could ever make in life. The lottery is designed for educated wealthy people to take advantage of false fantasies being fed to the poor, and it's a really huge mind trick because what they do is literally play with your head by asking you, "So, if you win the lottery, do you want your money in a lump sum, or do you want it over a 20 year period?"

Now, they could ask you after you win the lottery, when it's more relevant. But no, they ask you before, deliberately, because they know that the more that you make it real, in your mind, the more fantasizing you do. Psychologically, this makes you want to buy that ticket.

That really just comes from consumerism. Consumerism is built on the idea that most purchases are made from an emotional standpoint. They're made for emotional reasons. They're also compulsive purchases. People don't really sit and contemplate what they want to buy most of the time, they buy it right then.

So ultimately, that little stupid segment really made me angry, but that's neither here nor there. I had to bring that up, because these stereotypes are what's killing us and leaving us broke and leaving us hopeless and believing that investing must be for white people.

If you have a 401k in your job, especially if your company is matching any of that, max it out. Even before stashing acorns, and everything else I've taught you, go to your 401k.

Now 401ks are not necessarily always better than let's say IRA's, because IRA's are Individual Retirement Accounts, another tax deferred investment vehicle. Keep in mind that they are tax deferred, not tax exempt. Tax deferred, means that you're still going to pay taxes, you just pay later. But the 401k is a great tool, because companies provide that as an incentive and that's where you want to start building your wealth. If you max out your 401k, you're using your money; you're using Uncle Sam's money, and you're using your boss's money. That's a great way to invest and you get far more bang for your buck economically going that route than you get by investing on your own.

Rule number 5. Make somebody else a millionaire too. You know, just remember you know, kids have all the time in the world, and this investing is a legacy kind of scenario. You want to think of your family like a corporation. Your family is a business. Really you want to sort of think about to yourself,

"Maybe I can or can't make myself a millionaire, but I can certainly make my kids a millionaire."

That little two year old boy and that 10-year-old girl have so much time. They're going to need money one day as well. The fact of the matter is that basic investing programs for them, at an early age, can make a world of a difference.

When you talk about long term investing, one thing you may want to do is allow yourself to invest is to take your pay raises, and automatically put them back in the 401k plan, or put them in investing, just kind of commit yourself to whatever standard of living you're at now, and just say, even if my income increases, if I make more money from my job, or I make more money from my side hustle, or whatever the case may be, that the money is going to go toward investing. That way, your life can remain the same, and this natural growth in your income over time will allow you to build assets and build wealth.

That's one of the things that I did. I'll tell you guys the truth, I told you I like to enjoy money; I like to enjoy life and I never believed in torturing myself in order to get ahead and build wealth. I've always been an investor though. But I've always been an investor who felt that it was important to enjoy life.

But my biggest investment was actually time. I would invest my time into positioning myself by making sacrifices when I was young, so when I got a little bit older, I could live a better life, but even when I was 23, and I was studying seven to eight hours a day. I would put in my hours of studying and then I would spend a few hours of relaxing and doing whatever the heck I wanted.

So, what I did financially was, think about how I wanted my money to grow. So, I made my first investment of time. Even if you don't have a nickel in your pocket, you can invest time; you have a cell phone, you have access to the internet. Invest time, and realize that when you're investing that time, you're investing a financial asset.

Your time is worth money. That's why your boss pays you by

the hour or by the week or whatever. So, I invested time in entrepreneurship and then I created another stream of income. Now here's what happened. When I became more of an entrepreneur, I wasn't making a whole lot of money. First of all, I was losing money actually.

Then I started making money, I wasn't making a ton. I was making $300 this month, maybe $500 the next month, maybe a thousand the next month. But here's the thing. When I was making that extra money, two things happened. Number one, the financial physics of my income changed dramatically. Instead of being in my old life, where I was waiting for, you know I'd wait a whole year to get a three, 4% raise, I suddenly had a situation where I can increase my income by 20-30% in a month or two just by making the right business moves.

It's almost like the difference between plowing your field with human labor versus someone buying you an industrial size machine, that has the power of 5,000 human beings or whatever, it was a whole different level of possibility that came from thinking in an entrepreneurial stand point. Then also, I was then able to take the money I made from my job and enjoy that.

I could take that and buy whatever I wanted, live however I wanted. Because now, when it came to building my nest egg, I had this extra stream of income, that became my investment capital. That became my investment base. I was taking that money and investing it to build my long-term nest egg.

I'm not sure when I became a millionaire on paper, but I'm going to say, maybe it was around 2010, something like that, and when I hit that point, I still had to be kind of an investor, because, when you first become a millionaire, if your journey is anything like mine, you'll feel illiquid. Like it'll be like your business, and your business will finally be worth a million dollars, but it'll still be a small business.

Small businesses, require lots and lots of cash flow, lots and lots of economic food. We were making a dollar, and I had to put the dollar right back in. There was still a sacrifice there, but, the dynamics changed over time. That's what I would tell you guys to do, is sort of see income and wealth as something where there are a million different ways to skin that cat.

You don't have to think of it as "Okay, I'm going to live like a regular person and just take my little regular person paycheck and do what I can with that." When you get together with family, anything becomes possible, especially if you've got a family where five of you all are trained at a high level. If I wanted my family to be really wealthy, here's what I'd do.

I would challenge the family to do the Black Entrepreneurship Challenge. For a year, we would go through entrepreneurship training or boot camp style training where we're talking and we're learning about entrepreneurship on a regular basis. When you get to the end of that year, and you've got five people in the family who are all thinking entrepreneurially, then suddenly the whole world opens up to you and you realize just how much opportunity there is out there.

Now, let's jump back about specifics one more time. Here's exactly, how much you'd have to invest assuming a 7% return on investment, so it's a lot more conservative than the assumption we saw earlier. But this chart shows how much a person would have to invest in a diversified portfolio earning an average of 7% in order to be a millionaire by the time they hit the age of 65. Because, if you know how to hustle, you know how to position yourself right, those numbers might not apply to you.

For example, let's use $4168 as the number for the age of 45. 48 times 12 is $48,000 a year. Yes, that's an average income for an average American, but I guarantee you this: if you invest in education and you invest in entrepreneurship, that number goes up. Then you're playing a different game. Think about it, if you're a 20-year-old, and you're making the average monthly income of a 20-year-old, you only have to save about 13% of your income if you want to be a millionaire by the age of 65. 20-25 year-olds, pat yourselves on the back because you just won the lotto. You can be a millionaire by the age of 65 if you take these very basic steps.

Now you get to the age of 40, where you're not young anymore, but you're not old, but you have to move because time is running out. Well, a 40-year-old would have to save $1465 which is 35% of their income. The pressure grows, but again, I would say, if you have a double earning household, or you have a family that says, I'm only making $4000 now, but I want to get that up to six, things can shift.

Well guess what, you can hit that $1465 number and not change your lifestyle one bit. You don't have to change anything about how you live, how you make your money or how you spend your money. Sorry you have to change how you make your money but not how you spend your money.

Now when you get up to the 50s, it starts to get a little tough. The number grows to 94% of income because, if you're 50 and you waited this long, it's not over for you. You can always change the parameters and you can always retire a little bit later; you can always increase your income, but a 50-year-old, or a 55-year-old, would have to break out of the box in order to make this work. There's no way for example, you look at 55, $7800 is 188% of your income, you can't save 188% of your income, you can't do that, right?

The only option a 55-year-old might have, if they're trying to become a millionaire by 65 is they have to increase their income. Again, that's where entrepreneurship might come into play. Maybe you could retire a little bit later, maybe you could set your standard a little lower, and say, "Ah, you know, I don't need a million, maybe, three quarters of a million might work."

You can increase your income. Those are the three ways that a 55-year-old who hasn't saved for retirement can get caught up. You'd either have to increase your income, you would have to retire a little bit later or you have to set your standards a little bit lower. One of those three things would have to apply, or a combination of all three.

What I would say to, those of you who are under the age of 50, and most of you probably are is don't wait. Do not copy the investing behavior of the average American in this country, because, the average American in this country is going to financial hell in a hand basket.

The average American has ruined themselves economically, and what they are doing, is they're in a situation where they're just hoping for the best. They're just assuming that everything is just going to find a way to work out. I'm not making fun of these people at all, I'm just saying, if you don't have to be in that category, why do it?

Because the amount of money that they're talking about here, that you'd have to save every month is from say the age of 25 I mean, that $442 yeah, it's not easy, but, I know a lot of people that spend that much on their car notes, most people I know spend it at least twice that much on rent, and so ultimately, just shifting your thinking as early as possible makes a difference. If you can't do it for yourself, at least save that to your kids and your grandkids.

Talk to them about this. The other thing is to make sure that you're taking care of retirement because retirement is kind of an interesting space. It's where you're spending maybe 20 or 25 years of life, where you have to figure out how to get by with no income, or very little income. Now, you got Social Security, which gives you a little bit, maybe some retirees work part-time, some people have their 401ks and IRAs and other investment vehicles that kind of help supplement their income.

Some people are able to go live with their children and things like that. We tend to take care of our seniors in our community, white folks are a little bit interesting with their senior citizens, I've seen them throw them all out and put them in a home. I think that's crazy. Black people don't typically do that as much. But some of y'all might have some trifling kids. So, if that's who you are, I give you my condolences.

At the end of the day, when you're thinking about this retirement thing, just know that it's real. I've heard a lot of people say that it's silly for black people to save for retirement or put money on social security because we don't live long enough and all that. I say, yeah, I know that's true, you might die before you're 70 or 75, or 65 or whatever, but, you know what else? You might live. So, if you do live, then you want to be prepared; you want be protected and you don't want to just be out there with no plan.

So that is pretty much a straight forward blue print. I see becoming a millionaire by a certain time as very straight forward in the sense that it's not hard for me to explain it to you.

We just have to get over the myths. The myths are, I'm going to get a record deal, or I'm going to get into the NBA, or I'm going to join this multi-level marketing thing. No disrespect to multi-level marketing, but I don't know a lot of multi-level marketing millionaires to be honest with you, nor day traders or lotto winners.

The hardest part is dispelling the myths and helping people find intelligent and responsible ways to build that wealth, and understand the accumulation process. The hard part is that while it's straight forward, it is a long road.

You know, it's just like me trying to explain to you how to walk from Chicago to Las Vegas. It's easy to explain it; I say, here's the GPS and here's the map. Vegas is west, just keep going west and you're going to get there. But the question is how are you going to get there?

And if you don't start now, what are you doing with that time when you're not being productive? Meaning, if you're not invested in preparing for the future, what are you doing with that money? And what other things are you doing with that money that could be used for something that's more meaningful for your family.

I'm not saying that you can't still enjoy your money. I'm saying that you have to make sure that your investing is equal on the priority list to all the other things that you're doing.

You know, if you're spending money on anything with your

kids, make sure that you are teaching kids about wealth. I've told parents to keep doing what you're doing with your kids, just put entrepreneurship coaching on the same par as going to football camp, or on the same par as sending them to cheerleading camp every year.

These are fundamentals that they need to know in order to be successful. Same as you as an adult, when it comes to investing your money, and putting your money aside for you, and protecting your future, put them on the same par as going to IHOP every couple of days or whatever it is that you do with your money.

Let me use yet another illustration to draw this out for you. If a woman took the money that she spends on beauty and makeup and just said, *I'm going to make sure I invest the same amount in my future as I invest on my head*, then that woman has created an opportunity to generate income. In other words, she has made a commitment to spending as much money making sure that she's financially stable as she has in looking good. Of course, I am not just picking on the ladies. The same is true for black men.

If you did that, then you would have a whole lot of black female millionaires in this country. Point. Blank. Period.

And guys, we're not off the hook either, we waste our money on all kinds of ridiculous stuff. When I wrote my book *Financial Love Making*, and I was analyzing and interviewing couples, it amazed me as to how differently we think about money across gender lines.

When it came down to what they did with their money, most of the time, the financial tragedies actually came from the men. From men's irresponsible behaviors with their disposable income to not being good stewards of their credit. A lot of times, I warn black men, in particular, about the four vices.

Too often, we are getting caught up in activities that can ruin us financially and it often revolves around sex, drugs, alcohol and gambling. Now, before you call me judgmental or too pious, these four trends were derived from in-depth conversations, surveys, and research. This is not to say that all black men are culpable, but it is to suggest that we can often trace many of our financial shortcomings to one, if not more, of these common things.

So, yes, we all have our vices, but we also have traits and characteristics that make us great. One of those is the ability to reinvent ourselves and to change our behaviors. At the end of the day, everybody has their demons and everyone has their weaknesses, myself included.

What you do with *your money*, is often an emotional process. It can be quite irrational or even an illogical process, even for the most logical and rational of persons. Dr. Andrew Lowe, Professor at MIT, actually said that spending money and receiving money affects your brain in the same way as cocaine. Imagine that: We are constantly chasing an elusive high! However, we have to position ourselves to control our money and not the other way around.

So literally, you sometimes you make bad financial decisions because you're economically high. You're financially high. You're just in the mall, and the outfit looks good, and the music is playing, and you're caught up in some sort of emotional trance that leads you to part with your money. That's why, a lot of times, one way to keep from spending is to keep your money where it's tough to get to.

You know, if your money is in your stock portfolio and it's going to take three days for it to be released, then you're less likely to let that money go, in an impulsive decision because you have to wait three days in order to make the purchase.

So again, I would compare it to sex, imagine if people had to wait three days to decide if they wanted to have sex with someone, then the world's population would drop by about 40%. Because a lot of people, maybe some of you all have had babies with people where you were thinking "My God, what was I thinking?"

Regardless of the situation or the circumstance, once that

child is born, he/she is your responsibility. With the wealth of knowledge that you have gained and the potential you have, ensure that your child's financial future is secure.

CHAPTER 8

YOU ARE A MILLIONAIRE: NOW WHAT?

Don't let the title of this chapter startle you. I am not proposing that simply reading Chapters 1-7 will make you a millionaire. However, I am hopeful and optimistic that you will actively pursue and acquire a millionaire status. I wanted to include this chapter because some of us tend to stop setting goals once we have achieved a major milestone. Now that you know how to get it and keep it, what is your action plan after you have acquired that first million?

When you first start your business and you start succeeding, you'll have a lot of people that are going to want things from you. They're almost never going to show up and offer you things. 99 times out of 100, they're asking for something. Asking, asking, asking. It doesn't mean that you don't want to do it, it's just that you can give away so much of yourself that there's nothing left for you or anyone else.

My challenge to you is to be careful and make thoughtful decisions because it's not just about you and your well-being.

Before you know it, there's nothing left for your kids. Nothing left for you. Nothing left to keep your peace of mind. Literally, you can feel little pieces of your brain being chipped away. Then, what'll happen is you'll do 100 things for 100 people then there'll be that 101st person who'll say, "I asked him to do something for me and he didn't do it. He ain't nothing."

You'll never get to the point where you can make everybody happy. That's like trying to drink the entire ocean. It doesn't mean you shouldn't keep trying, though, but it does mean that that does become a complication, especially once you become a person that's successful.

That's why I always tell people, "Don't brag about how much money you've got." I don't care if you're doing well or not. If you're doing well that's good, but don't brag about it. Don't go flossing and trying to drive the fanciest car or have the nicest whatever, including the biggest house and all of that because as soon as people see that, there's a natural human instinct. They're going to see you as a person they can go to get resources. People who you think are your friends, or who you thought really want to be around you because they like you, are actually around you because they think they might be able to get something from you. It doesn't mean everybody thinks that way. I'm not saying that at all. Let's say that you've got it like that. You go on vacation with your best friend and you drop $10,000 on the vacation. You say, "Hey, let's go to Hawaii together. I'll pay for it. It's my treat."

Because one day all of you will be multimillionaires, so you'll have it like that. Let's say you splurge and you go spend $10,000 taking your friend to Hawaii. Let's say your friend comes home and he needs $1,000 to pay the rent. He's going to be thinking, "Of course $1,000 is nothing to her because she just dropped $10,000 going to Hawaii, so why would it be a big deal for me to ask for $1,000?" Your friend may not understand that you do not want to spend your $1,000 to help him pay the rent. You might have wanted to use the money for something else. Do you understand? Also, another interesting thing that just came up in terms of this: A lot of people think that in order to build wealth you have to really think like a miser.

Some people perceive that you have to just act like you're broke all the time, never spend money on anything, count every penny, just be real anal about it. I don't believe that. I think that you can certainly enjoy your money. I think that's okay. I think you should. I just think that the key is moderation. The key is making sure that you always have some form of healthy investment habit, investment protocol, that allows you to build wealth as you spend money. You understand? For example, if you land on $1,000 I don't think you have to invest the whole $1,000 in order to build wealth. Basically, even 5% or 10% of that will make a huge difference in your life.

Anyway, one thing I want to mention to you guys, again, as we get started is I want to reiterate that if you are interested in staying in the class and you would like to join the Black Wealth Academy, you can join the Black Wealth Academy at the link I'm about to give you. I know I've mentioned it several times but this is something I definitely want to do because I know that it has value. I wouldn't offer it to you if it wasn't a tremendous value. It's better than anything you'll get on a college campus.

Here's the thing: as you implement all these ideas and this ambition that you have from what you learned in the boot camp, you've got to understand that you will, basically, end up in a scenario where you're going to have to be pushed to implement some of this. What we do with the academy is we help you through boot camp style learning to continue implementing what it is you plan to do.

We become almost like coaches, if you will. We hold you accountable, we push you. All that good stuff. That's important and here's why. I was talking to a Ph.D. student today and giving her advice on how to get done with her dissertation. Getting a Ph.D. is like being hazed if you're getting one from a tough school. Some people get these Ph.D. s that they can get on the weekends and all that. I'm not knocking it, but it's not the same process. Like in sororities or fraternities, you've got people that really went through the hell of pledging, then you've got people that sign a piece of paper and pay some money when they are 35. I'm not knocking it one way or the other, but it's a different process.

She was going through this horrible thing. I said, "When you're going through something like that, whether it's getting a Ph.D. or building a business or anything, you're almost always going to feel like a failure. You're almost always going to feel like you're never going to get to the finish line. You're almost always going to feel stressed out and frustrated and mad and feel like you're wasting your time." I said, "The key is to just shut down all of that if you can and focus on one simple idea. Just do a little bit every day, a little bit every day." Because wealth accumulation is consistent with other forms of accumulation, consistent with achievement accumulation. When a person has a long resume full of accolades and all that stuff, which I've got a decent little resume now because I'm 44, it's because I've been working hard.

All of those accolades reflect a culmination of little, tiny, day to day efforts over time. I can show you that I've been on national TV probably 3-400 times. I didn't go on it all at once. I didn't try to do it all in a week. I would just do one and then another one and then another one and then another one. Next thing I know, I've got 3-400. You understand? When you think about the accumulation of success, think about the incremental stages. Also, think like an investor. Always think like an investor. What does that mean? That means that anything that you put out, any resources that you're sharing, whether it's your time, your money, your love, your focus, your relationships, always think about it in terms of putting something in today that is going to get you a payoff or some benefit later on.

It is just not about a financial payoff though. It doesn't have to be financial. It has to be in terms of what they call utility. Utility and economics is basically your overall well-being or the quality of your life. That's the goal. Really, when you think about investing, you want to think about it in a holistic standpoint, not just in terms of money.

So, you may ask: "Dr. Watkins, when investing in someone else's business, if I invest $50,000 for 10%, does that mean if the company makes $10,000 a month, do I, as an investor, get $1,000 each month?"

Basically, being an investor at a certain percentage means you get a percentage of the profits. You also own a percentage of the revenue, but some of that revenue may go back into the company. What you probably want to do is talk to the owners about an understanding on how much of the revenue is a dividend, meaning you get to take it and go spend it on something else versus how much of that revenue is going to be utilized for reinvestment.

For example, with my company *Financial Juneteenth*, my brother and I started it. We try to own everything. We try to own everything we do unless we can't own it, meaning that we can't afford it or it's too risky or whatever. We try to own everything because we're thinking about our kid and grandkids. My brother hasn't even had kids, but we're planning for his children who are not yet born. We want them to be able to start the race with a head start. He's younger than me, by the way. He's 12 years younger than me. With *Financial Juneteenth,* we have an understanding that every time we get money, a certain percentage will go toward dividends. We give each other information on spending.

He'll tell me how much we spent on technology and how much we've spent on human capital and how much is left. He'll always take 10% of the total revenue and put it in retained earnings. That means that it's going in the bank. It's our stockpile. We're stacking cash so that when we get that next bright idea I can say, "Hey man, why don't we take $5,000 out of retained earnings and invest in this new project?"

You understand? You want to do that. You want to make that understanding in the beginning, though. Because companies and shareholders always fight. Managers and shareholders constantly fight over dividends because, basically, the company's bottom line is more important than anything else. If you aggregate that to a large corporation, let's say a multibillion dollar company, the dividend fight comes into play when you have a company that's growing really fast or when you have a growth stock, a growth company. You don't want to pay a lot of dividends because that's taking cash out of the company.

A growth company is a great place to put your money. If you have a company that's growing really fast, you don't want to take all that money and waste it. You want to put that money right back in, pump it right back in, raise more capital because by being a growth company, what that means is you have a lot of investment opportunities.

You have a lot of things you can put your money into that will get you more money later on. Growth companies are like flowers that need lots of water. Money is called liquidity for a reason. Money is like the water that you're watering the plant with. The plant is just sucking down all the water because it's growing so fast. It's got uses for all that water. There gets to be a point where the company's not growing anymore. The company might still be making money but it hits a different part of its life cycle, it can be what they call a cash cow. A cash cow is a company where all the businesses are pretty well defined and established.

There aren't many more growth opportunities. They've explored all the options that are out there. Basically, the company's generating tons and tons of revenue, but they don't have anything they want to invest in unless they go into a new industry or something like that. Sometimes you don't want that. What happens is there's usually a fight in a lot of these companies where these shareholders come back and they say, "Back when you were a young company and you were growing really fast, we wanted you to keep our money. We wanted you to take the profits and reinvest the profits because we knew you had growth opportunities and we knew you knew what to do with that money. But now you're a cash cow. Now you're doing good, you're bringing in revenue, keep doing that, but when you get that revenue, when you get that profit, give it to me. Pay me a dividend. Increase your dividend so I can take my money and put it elsewhere." I can either spend it, which means use it for consumption, or I can take it somewhere else and put it into another business.

If I own part of a railroad, a railroad is kind of a stable, almost borderline dying industry for the most part, it depends on how you look at it. When airplanes came along, railroads became less relevant so, basically, railroads, radio stations, things like that, tend to, maybe be cash cow kinds of companies. They're not really going to grow that much. You might take the money from your railroad stock or from the radio stock and put that into a dotcom. You may say, "You know what? The radio is doing okay but it's not going to grow much, but the internet is booming. I'm going to put some of my dividend money into a dotcom." That's what the conversation is about dividends so you want to really talk to your investors to talk to them about that.

Also, as far as reviewing financial statements, if you're investing in someone else's company, you probably want to ask them who is your accountant? Maybe we can agree on who the accountant is going to be and we can also agree that the accountant is going to send everybody a monthly report so everything is transparent. You want transparency, especially when it comes to your damn money. You always want transparency. In fact, just today, and I'm feeling passionate about this issue just because of some things I saw this week that bothered me, you should always have information about where your money is going, period.

Transparency should be something they understand. If they have a hard time with transparency, then you probably should not invest your money with that person.

I had a very interesting discussion about that with minister Louis Farrakhan when we were in Arizona at an economic development gathering. He had nine economists, myself and eight other people, in a room. We were talking about a long term economic plan for black America. The Nation of Islam is comprised of some talented brothers who are very smart and very sharp. They do research. They have Ph.D. s in their organization. They were taking notes on what we were talking about. One of the things that I mentioned to the minister, which he actually knew already was related to economics.

I said, "When you're gathering other people's money, for example, we talked about the building of a Black bank (Of course, I can't divulge everything that happened, but that is one of the things we talked about)." I said, "You have to make sure that you have complete transparency when it comes to other people's money. You can't take people's money and then not answer questions if they ask you about the money." Here's the thing though. The minister, he answered that very well. He mentioned that after the Million Man March, he said, "We took all the money that we made. We had an independent accounting review of all this money. Every penny was accounted for and all the information was made public."

The point of the matter is that when you start something with somebody, you take other people's money or you're giving money, understand that it becomes a more serious game at that point. You're putting your relationship on the line, number one, if you're investing with a friend or a family member, but then also you could be putting your freedom on the line. You're taking money from other people. You mismanage the money, you take a little bit of the money out of your business bank account and use it to pay to get your hair and nails done or use it to pay your rent, when that catches up with you then suddenly you become a criminal.

When you become a criminal, you end up like that poor brother who used to work with Bishop Eddie Long. I can't remember his name. This brother used to go around the country and go on TV shows and talk about being a young investment guru. People talked about how brilliant he was. I think he was brilliant. He's very smart. But unfortunately, he collected a lot of money from these churches and they invested in his project and suddenly people weren't able to get their money. Suddenly they were calling his office and he wasn't answering the phone.

Here's the thing: He's living in a multimillion dollar apartment. He's driving fancy cars. His wife is going on expensive vacations with him. People were like, "Where's this money going?" The SCC gets involved, the securities and exchange commission, and next thing you know he's got federal charges on him. The thing about federal charges is that you don't want to play with the government when it comes to that money. That's why I don't take money from the government. I just don't. I'm going to work and build and create systems. I recently met with my accountant for seven hours talking about where all the money was going. When you own everything yourself and you're not in crazy complex business relationships, it's a little easier to figure things out.

However, if you take money from the government, they treat you worse than if you were stealing someone else's money; in some cases, the penalties are so severe that they treat you worse for stealing money than they would if you murdered somebody. That's a fact. I have friends who are in federal prison right now, I'm talking about smart people. There's one lady I met who literally used to be friends with Michelle Obama. Michelle was her girl. "Hey Michelle. How you doing, girl?" They were that tight. She got caught up in something that involved a government grant and next thing you know, she's going to prison for nine years. She's going to be away from her husband and away from her children. The government does not give a damn about what life you had going on before you went to prison.

You know what else? Guess how many of her Harvard-educated, Michelle Obama politically connected friends are calling her back now that she's been hit with the label of felon? Zero. She's told me, "Dr. Watkins, nobody's talking to me now. None of my so-called friends are even talking to me anymore." Be very, very careful when it comes to money. You just have to be really, really careful. I could just tell you more stories. Bernard Madoff. Do you remember Madoff? The guy who ran the Ponzi scheme. He made a lot of money but, apparently, the federal government decided he was running a Ponzi scheme.

They sent him to prison for 30, 40 years. Do you know his secretary also went to prison? His secretary. I think that they just concluded that she benefited, too. Maybe she covered up some records or whatever, but I just have a hard time imagining that his secretary would really know all the details and the illegalities of what they were doing, but maybe I'm wrong. Maybe she knew more. It's just a mess.

Another example, see I'm coming up with all these examples. I knew a drug dealer who had relatives that would help him launder the money and stuff like that. Do you know, when they sent him to prison on a RICO charge?

They sent him to prison for 14 life sentences all over the money. It was all about the money. They didn't have any murders on him. They found him with no drugs. It was all about the money and the conspiracy. That's what the whole case was. They also sentenced his mother, his sister, and his brother, and several of his friends just because they touched the money. Just be very, very careful when it comes to money. The government don't play on that stuff.

Another way to maintain your wealth is via international trading and stock exchanges. A lot of the American style markets, the New York Stock Exchange, are owned by foreigners. The Chinese are notorious savers. They do a very good job of saving their money. What they do is they end up buying up just big chunks of the United States.

Make no mistake about it, pretty soon we will be deeply in debt to China in so many ways. Our slogan is "Don't climb the corporate ladder. Build one." Black people have to build things. The easiest way to be a boss in this world, the easiest way to be a boss is to create something and make yourself the boss of it. You know how you were little and you'd create a little clubhouse and you'd say, "I'm the king of this club"?

It probably seemed weird but maybe you were onto something. The thing at that point is you have to figure out how am I going to get people to want to be in this club? That's what I did. When I started off doing the stuff that I do now, understand this. When I first started off as an intellectual public whatever I am, nobody knew who I was.

You're going to laugh about this. I used to be on this list serve with other scholars back when I was younger. I used to write my articles. I used to think, "How can I get people to read my articles? I know they're good but no one will read them." I didn't know how to get into the media, didn't know how to get wide distribution on anything that I put out. I would write these articles and I would put the articles ... The list serve was basically like email where everybody would email the same address and everybody got the same message, back in those days before Facebook. I would write my little articles. I would put them on the list serve, hoping that people would read them.

I'd get a couple people who would write back and say, "That was really good. That was really nice." Then I had people, though, who were annoyed, who were just like, "What is this guy doing? Who is he? Why are you bothering me?" Then I finally started getting on TV. Again, I believe you should do this. When you're building your brand for yourself or for your company, tell people what you're doing. Always tell them what you're up to so the people in your space know that you're active, they know what you're all about. They identify you with an idea. I started telling people, "I'm going to be on," first it was local TV, local radio, then it became national. "I'll be on

CNN, blah, blah, blah." Unfortunately, that's when I learned a little more about things like jealousy. I had some colleagues who were just like, "I don't want to hear that shit." Eventually, I got booted off the list.

The person who ran the list serve was an academic at Rutgers University. Once she reached out to me and said: "I'm sure you have plenty of other places to put your work so we're going to ask you to leave the list." My feelings were hurt. I was sad. I was like, "What did I do? I was just telling people what I'm doing." Maybe I was a nuisance, but the thing was when I first got started with writing, I didn't have an outlet. I didn't have anywhere to really go in terms of putting myself out there. There was no big deal to be around Dr. Boyce Watkins and to work with him because nobody cared about that.

The thing was I would take ownership of things. I would create things and say, "This may not be anything, but it's mine. I own this." I start a website. "This is my website." I start a company, "This is my company." The company got no revenue, no buildings, no resources, not even a cardboard box, but dammit it's mine and I'm proud of that. What I found was that I felt good about owning something. I said, "If I can make this thing worth something, if I can make this go kart move, then this is going to be mine. I won't have to share this. I won't have to beg anybody for anything. If I can learn how to make a movie, if I want to be a movie star, I can be a movie star. I've just got to get people to watch the movie."

I took that approach like the little kid who creates the tree house and says, "I'm the king of this tree house." At that point, how do you get people to want to be in the tree house? I started off in my little apartment in Syracuse, New York by myself living all alone. Spent 99% of my time by myself. I moved there because I wanted to be in a place where I could focus on working hard. All my 30s, all I did was work. I was building these things, doing these things, trying to get the stuff off the ground. Slowly but surely good things started to happen. It was a matter of accumulation. Every day, I just worked really hard. I kept a spreadsheet. I used to keep a spreadsheet where on the spreadsheet I would give myself one point for everything I did that got me closer to my long-term goal, even if I didn't know what the goal was. I knew one fundamental idea. The fundamental idea is that if you invest your time in working hard at something, something is going to change.

Something good is probably going to happen if you continue to move forward in the same direction. If I keep walking north and I don't stop, then eventually I am going to walk into the ocean. If I go west, I'm going to eventually get to California or Seattle or something. I just focus on taking those little steps every day instead of setting my goals based on whether or not I was successful or not.

I didn't want to do that because I knew that sometimes you try to do things and it doesn't work out, but you've got to keep trying. Instead of focusing on how many successes I had, I would focus on how many efforts I put out. I was like, "If I tried to do 10,000 things to be successful, then at least a couple hundred of those things are going to do something good for my life. I just don't know which of these 10,000 is going to work but I'm just going to do them all."

I was setting my goal each month based on the number of efforts, number of investments I made in what I was trying to do. I had a little money to invest so my job became my first source of capital. I also had time to invest. I would clear out my time. I didn't waste my time with foolishness. I didn't waste my time with dumb stuff. I didn't waste my time with friends that I didn't want to have around me. I didn't waste my time dealing with people that were going to just derail me from what I was trying to do. I didn't waste my time running around with random women. Men get in so much trouble with that kind of thing.

I focused on my goal. I fell in love with my dream. My dream kept me company even when nobody else was around, even when the world had bought me out and didn't care about what

I was doing or where I was at, whether I lived or died that day. You know what happened? Slowly but surely things started to work out. Slowly but surely things started to get better. Slowly but surely that little club I created that nobody cared about, that got me booted out of this little group, suddenly people wanted to be part of that club. People who I admired started reaching out to me.

People started reaching out and saying, "I want to know that guy. Who is that guy? Let me talk to him. Can you get him on the phone?" Every one of them. I didn't reach out to any of them. I didn't go and say, "Hi, my name is Boyce. I'm trying to get ahead. Can you hook me up, man?" I didn't do all of that. I just focused on building and I focused on making tiny investments and before you knew it, I had a club that I built that suddenly people wanted to be a part of. Do you understand?

Build your own club and sustain it, make yourself the boss, and work hard at it every day. Eventually, people will come up. A young person will come up and say, "I want to be like you when I grow up. How can you mentor me? Can I work for you? Can I be down with you? Can I just be your friend? Can I just be around you?" It's an amazing experience. That's the honest to god truth about what I went through. I hope it wasn't TMI but I hope it helps you if you feel like what you have isn't worth anything. You have to make it worth something. You build your go kart and you put an engine in it and you make that sucker go.

Also, be receptive to new ideas. Once you make that first million, don't get too comfortable or rest on your laurels, as they say. Literally when a lightning bolt hits my head, I have to write down the idea because I really want to share this theory with people. I'm sharing with you guys first. If I say it wrong, forgive me, because it's literally coming off the dome. I think that people should consider becoming Uber drivers as you make the transition to get off the corporate plantation. Let me tell you why. Uber is a gold mine for so many Black people all across the country. South side Chicago, a place where jobs are just very hard to find, there are people I know making between $1,000 and $1,500 driving for Uber, working flexible schedules, or working with Uber in the time that they're not at their job.

If you're trying to raise capital for your business, something like that could be a great way to add money to your bottom line. Maybe letting somebody else use your car to be an Uber driver, I don't know if that's legal or not, but if you've got that relative who's sitting on the couch, got nothing to do, and you've got a car, you say, "Okay, go drive Uber and we'll split the money."

What that does is that brings in the extra cash which allows you a lot more freedom to do the things you want to do. It makes it easier to pay certain bills. It also gives you a source of capital for that first business. Not just financial capital, but also capital in terms of time. Why? Because let's say I'm working, I'm making $50K a year on the plantation, I hate the job, and I want to switch and I want to leave. The job sucks. I want to do something different but I'm not quite ready to run a business on my own.

Maybe I transition into becoming an Uber driver and my income remains the same but the game changer is that I have flexibility now. I can be driving or between rides I can be doing business on the phone. I can come home and work all day on my business on the days where I need to be with my business. The Uber company isn't going to ask me, "Hey boy, where are you at today? You're supposed to be at work." They're not going to do that to me. I could drive extra on the weekends to make up for the fact that I have to do business from 9 to 5. I think that's a game changer. I'm dead serious. I really think Uber can be one of the keys to getting millions of Black people off the corporate plantation.

I believe it so much that I wish that they had an affiliate program to recommend people to become drivers because I would be recommending thousands of Black people to go drive an Uber. I've interviewed Uber drivers. You go to my YouTube channel. You type Boyce Watkins and Uber. You'll see an interview I did with a brother. I was his first ride. I asked him, "Why'd you become a driver? What was the process like? How hard was it?" He told me that he had a friend who was doing it and his friend was making money so he decided to try it," and all this other stuff. I've noticed that, in Chicago, especially on the south side, 90% of my Uber drivers are white. Black, sorry. I don't know where white came from.

90% of my Uber drivers are Black. Look into that as a way to make some extra money either in conjunction with the money you're getting from the plantation or as a substitute, as a slow transition. That's what you have to do. You're not going to have a company that's going to go from zero to 60 overnight most of the time. If you're looking to get off the plantation, maybe moving to a more flexible job, even if you make slightly less money, it could be part of your transition process. Get that free time. Remember, time is more valuable than money. Don't ever underestimate the importance of your time.

In fact, you're a CEO now. Your time is certainly more valuable than your money. I know a whole lot of people who went to school who were never educated. Also, remember that there's a difference between education and knowledge. As a Black person, knowledge is going to benefit you more because knowledge will help you become a more authentic and more empowered Black person.

Just understanding things like how to be a good husband and a good father, understanding the needs of your community, how to build a business, how to raise your children a certain way, that kind of education and knowledge can be far more valuable than what you learn in school.

Think about it. When we go to these white schools, they have us reading Edgar Allan Poe and learning all these Eurocentric concepts. It's not to say that that's all a waste of time. I'm not saying that at all. But we've got to understand that knowledge and education can come from all sources, not just from a school. As far as I'm concerned, I'm talking to a brilliant man. "I need education for you and your family. May I reach out to you about more classes?" Absolutely. Send me an email, join the Academy.

If anybody's interested in just looking at all the classes in the Black business school, we could really use your help. We're really pushing to make this thing strong. We're actually going to have a fundraising and membership drive pretty soon. It's going very well. It's growing. We have thousands of members now. I really want this thing to hit a critical mass of impact in the Black community.

I'm literally going to dedicate nearly all of my money, all of my time to making this thing go. I'm fighting with my friends who are in academia to get them to come over to the dark side, which is the good side in our case, dark skin. That's what I mean. To come over with us. Most of them are actually receptive. Most of them are looking for something better to do with their lives. I'm saying, "You need to be home. You need to go natural. You need to be back with your people. You need to go Black." They understand this. It's not a hard argument.

The goal is to eventually offer more classes that are directly related to the things that you need in order to be successful and empowered. Why?

I understand that. "Ballin' on the budget." That's the story of the Black man's life. You know what? Lionel, I will say that you can invest whatever you want. I think $5 or $10 a month is okay. If that's what everybody agrees on then go for it. If somebody invests more, than you want to make sure they have a bigger cut and all that stuff. You've got to have somebody that can do the math to make sure they get what they deserve. I don't see why $5 or $10 a month is a bad number. Remember this, too, there are things that we spend $5 a day on that we could easily cut out of our budget and use that money for investing.

You'd be amazed how much money you could save just by taking the spare change out of your pocket and putting it into a jar every day. That'll actually pile up to a decent amount of money. I've been doing that for years. I still do that to this day. I'll go and I'll have thousands of dollars in this big spare change jar just from, literally, every time coming home having the habit of emptying my pockets. Other things, like if you go to McDonald's for lunch every day or if you go to Starbucks, add up. Starbucks coffee is really expensive. You spend $5 to $6 on Starbucks coffee. That can literally add up. If somebody took the money they spent on Starbucks coffee every day and put it in the stock marker for 35, 40 years, they would have well over half a million dollars, maybe as much as $700,000.

That's wealth. That's capital. Imagine if your child started life and they've got $700,000 in a trust fund to invest in their business. That literally would mean that the fact that you cut Starbucks out of your life in order to prepare for your children, that literally could mean that they could go their whole life without ever having a boss. They could go their whole life without ever having to work for anybody but themselves. You can literally change a life by cutting Starbucks or McDonald's value meals out of your budget. That's how powerful capital accumulation can be if you do it consistently.

However, I don't think you should live a totally spartan life if you don't want to. In fact, I think it makes investing less fun if everything is serious all the time, if everything is always hard. I don't want a life that's not enjoyable. I think you can do both. I think the key is balance. What happens is people don't have balance. When I was in college, I made straight A's. I was absolutely, positively a good college student even though I was a very, very bad high school student. The reason I was a torrentially good college student was not because I was smarter than my classmates, it was for two reasons.

One, because I think like an investor. I was thinking, at the age of 20, what can I do with my life right now that's going to make my life easier when I'm 40? What can I do right now that's going to make life easier when my baby daughter grows up and becomes a full-grown human being and needs something from her daddy? That was one thing.

The other thing was that a lot of people lived under this myth that in order for me to make straight A's I had to just not have any fun. I told them, I said, "I think that's the dumbest thing I've ever heard. I have more fun than most of my friends largely because I'm not under any stress because I do my studying in advance. I just knock it out. I don't wait til the night before the test where I can't get any sleep." I hate that feeling. Staying up all night, taking No Doze, drinking all this coffee and the coffee's not even working, haven't took a shower and you're still not ready for the test.

Trying to remember all this information because you tried to shove a month's worth of information in your brain overnight. That doesn't work. At 18, I realized, I said, "If I'm going to get ready for the test, if i study hard now, three weeks before the test, that's just the same as me studying hard the night before the test. The only difference is if I do it now I'll have three weeks for the information to sink in. I'll get ahead of the class because I'll know the information a week or two before everybody else." When the teacher would say, "We're having a test in a month. It's going to cover these six chapters." I would literally jam. I called it jamming. People did cramming. I would joke and say, "I'm going to jam." What I would do is after the previous test, I would literally read all the chapters in advance that I was going to have to read for the next test.

I would come into class. I literally knew everything before the teacher taught it which made me look like a genius even though I only knew something that everybody else is going to know in five minutes after the teacher explained it to them. The teacher saw me as the best student.

Also, I was ready for the test. When it came time for the exam, I've already read the chapters two or three times. The information has sunk in. The night before the test was just a review session for me. I'd just be going through my notes looking around. I'd be on the basketball court the day of finals. People would be like, "Why are you on the basketball court? You've got finals." I was like, "I've already prepared for finals.

I'm ready." I made A's on all my finals. My point here is that in life in general, and that philosophy, I kept that with me in everything I do. To this day, I'm still the same guy.

I would say in life in general, pick up the skills, but don't think you have to let go of the thrills. In fact, the thrills are better when you have the skills. You work hard now, you do things now that no one else will do so that later on you can do things that other people can't do. Just think of it that way. Think of it as a balance framework, not as an all or nothing framework. I hope that's helpful to you.

Let me tell you about a method of sustaining your wealth that many people ignore and that is writing books. My dear friend and literary scholar, Dr. Tyra Seldon has a quote that really resonates with me, "A good book does not have an expiration date or a shelf life." This is true.

There are many of us who are subject matter experts (SME). Our life experiences and success equip us to share our experiences with others and a book is a great way to do that. Think about how you obtain information; I am pretty sure that books are one of your primary resources. Instead of reading someone else's book, what would it take for you to write your own? If it is marketed correctly, you will find that you have another stream of passive income. Your books also become a part of your legacy. Remember, books live on well after we die.

If the idea of writing a book seems too daunting, we offer a course in the Black Business School. If you go in there, you will find that we have a class that includes detailed information about writing books and, if you want, we can provide ongoing consultation. Dr. Tyra Seldon teaches the class and it includes curriculum about writing books, selling books, branding and more.

I believe that when you write books, you should publish things yourself. I'm also a big believer in creating your own publishing company or having things done independently. I'm not a big fan of going to these literary agents and hoping and praying that they give you an opportunity because 99 times out of 100 they don't. They don't pay attention to you. It's a waste of your time because you invest all this time going to meetings and following up with people when you could be spending that time building your own.

Anyway, with that being said, if I had a sci-fi book based on the Black community, I would literally ask myself, before you create the book: Who is my audience? I had a conversation with the filmmaker who made the film *Black Friday*, which is a great film about Black economic empowerment. We're actually going to serve as an affiliate and help them distribute that film. One of the things that we talked about was he said, "Before I made this film, I had to think carefully about who my audience is. Who's going to buy this film? Who's going to want to see it?" He said, "Then at that point I had to figure out how to get access to that audience. Where's that audience located?" I said, "I really like the way you think. A lot of filmmakers put the cart before the horse. They make the movie and then they figure out who's going to watch it. If you make the film the wrong way you're not going to have any demographic."

He talked about a guy who made a movie about the Black Christian church, but it was from an Atheist perspective. He said, "How many Black atheists do you know?" I said, "A couple, but not a whole lot. Not a critical mass. Not enough to sell a film." Anyway, if you're writing the book like that, I would ask myself, "What makes my book unique? What are the unique selling points? What things can I use as headlines on other content that will make people want to take a peak to see what this book is about?" Maybe your story is unique. Maybe you got shot nine times like 50 Cent and you came back to life after being shot nine times.

Being shot launched 50 Cent's whole career. Think about it, he'd repeat it 50 million times. "I got shot nine times, shot nine times." Maybe you have something in your story that makes you unique. Maybe you were illiterate until a certain age. Things like that. Then what you might do is, if you've got a book, you definitely want to have a Facebook Fan Page for you and for your book even if nobody's on it.

At that point, you've got to figure how to get people on it. I would also create regular content. I would have a YouTube channel. I would have a Twitter and Instagram and then a Facebook. You have all that stuff going then you populate it with content. I'm a big fan of content that doesn't take a lot of time. YouTube videos, short. I do a couple things that I love to do that doesn't take much time.

I love to do short YouTube videos. I love to do short audio clips. I have SoundCloud on my phone, a SoundCloud app. I would show it to you but I'm not going to waste your time showing you. You know what it looks like. A SoundCloud where I can literally record a segment, almost like a radio segment. I hit load and boom, it appears on my SoundCloud file. Then I do a short video. I hit load and it goes to my YouTube channel. I have a Facebook app and I hit load and it goes to my Facebook page. If you follow me on Facebook, what you will see is that literally, for about 45 seconds I talk to you guys, I did a short video about my Grambling sweater. Why did I do it? I don't know. I just felt like I wanted to give a shout out to Grambling.

It's cool. It fits my brand. You know me as a guy who supports the Black community, who cares about the Black community. I was like, "I'm going to talk about this Grambling sweater." You see how the fun and the business can be merged in a really cool way? But of course, as I'm talking about the Grambling sweater, I'm also going to mention, "Check out the business school. I think you guys will like it." You're seeing me. I am a brand. Every person that's a public figure is some kind of a brand. You have to be conscious of that, right?

I would just find little ways to talk about things that link to the core. The core is that you're a sci-fi writer who wrote this cool sci-fi book for the Black community. Everything would come back to that. Everything that you do you could say, "Hi, my name is," and I lost your name. I'm so sorry, brother. You could say, "Hi, my name is, fill in the blank, I am the author of, fill in the blank," then you give people the information. Then at the end, you say, "Thank you very much. I am blank, author of blank. You can find out more at www.blank.com." In a way, what you're doing is you're giving things to the world, but everything has to be sponsored.

All media is sponsored. Whenever you watch a football game, like the brother who was watching the Cardinals and the Vikings, that football game is brought to you by somebody. Verizon, brought to you by Ford. In this game, in this Black entrepreneurial game, you don't have Ford and Verizon sponsoring you most likely. You're sponsoring yourself. What is bringing this to you? If you wrote a book, then this is being brought to you by the book, blah, blah, blah. You don't say it like that but that's what you're doing because, hopefully, you have a model at some point where a certain percentage of the people who see you will like you and want to be connected to your brand on a more deeper level. That was wrong. You know what I mean. On a deeper level. I didn't need to say more deeper level. In a deeper way, right?

Effectively, if you want to understand the crux of a lot of how I do things, that's what it is. When I get on the internet and I really look like I'm having fun, it's because I'm really having fun. I'm really connecting to what I know. I know Black people. I know the Black community. I'm just in the Black community. I'm a scholar which, I think, gives me uniqueness. I have the ability to, maybe, take a conversation and elevate it to a place that adds value to people. I'm always thinking like a giver. That's the key. That's the key to everything. You must always think like a giver because the more you give to the world, the more the world will want to give back to you.

Everybody isn't going to give. I have people that, if I mention the Black business school and I tell them the class isn't free, they think I'm a crook. "You're trying to rob the Black community, blah, blah, blah." They think every Black business owner is a crook. That's going to happen. There are people that, I think, look at that and they say, "Gosh, Dr. Boyce has given me so much. Maybe I can support what he's working on.

Maybe I can be a part of this." It's not like you're not going to benefit. The classes, you literally save thousands of dollars because I give you information that would cost a lot of money to obtain elsewhere. It took me a lot of years and a lot of money to figure these things out.

You get the value there, but even if you didn't, by virtue of the fact that you are giving so much to the world, you'll find that your biggest fans, your biggest supporters will want to give you something back. They'll have your back when you need them to and then you'll make enough money to keep operating and keep functioning and doing what you're doing. That's always been my goal. I never cared much about being rich. I think wealth is important, though, because I'm having some bigger visions and dreams about things I want to do.

I want to buy a big plot of land and some buildings and actually have a Black tech incubator where I can actually get money to fund small Black tech businesses, let the incubator take a percentage ownership, and bring the people in and actually have them around other tech entrepreneurs so that they can develop the next Black Facebook, the next Black whatever. Building wealth is important to me for that reason, but for the most part I never wanted to just have a bunch of money floating around.

I take most of my money and I put it right back into the business because I'm literally just living and enjoying my life and having fun and giving to the community in a way that sustains the giving. If you don't sustain it, if you don't have money coming back in, because maybe you care nothing about money or whatever, then you're stuck in this situation where you're not going to be able to keep doing what you're doing. If I don't have money coming in I can't keep doing what I'm doing because I'm going to have to go, eventually, down the street to the white man and ask him to give me a job because I've got to feed my kids. Do you understand?

Ultimately, that's what you want to aim for. Just keep giving. Find out what your brand is. What's unique about this? I think being a Black sci-fi writer is pretty cool. It's pretty rare. You could literally have things out there where you just say, "I am Black sci-fi writer John Smith." I'm so sorry I don't have your name, man. I forget stuff very, very fast. You have to forgive me for that. I'm good at figuring things out but I'm not always good at remembering things. My sister's the doctor. She remembers everything.

Let's shift gears and talk about something that may make some of you uncomfortable, but it fits in with the theme of this book and this chapter. Dr. Claude Anderson speaks frequently on the need for reparations. People will often ask me if I agree.

I agree that we have a right to reparations. I don't know if we need reparations nor will we be paid reparations but you should never say never because things always change. Five years ago, I didn't think anybody would ever care about Black men being shot down by the cops. That was my biggest gripe. I used to be so mad because I said, "These Black men are being killed and nobody's saying anything. Nobody cares." Then suddenly everybody's talking about Black Lives Matter. It really started with Trayvon and all this other stuff.

Things can change overnight. A lot of times, you want to pursue things because you're laying the groundwork for what could be an opportunity later on. You know how they say opportunity knocks once and when it knocks you better have your bags packed? Sometimes you've got to pack your bags even if you don't think opportunity's coming to the door. But you have your bag packed just in case because you don't want opportunity to knock and for you not to have your bags packed. I would say that, when it comes to conversations like reparations, I say, "Yeah, let's keep having them." Let's keep getting in the faces of people who owe us money and telling them, "You owe us. Here's proof." Let's keep spreading awareness that reparations are owed.

How can you steal from a group of people for 250 years and act like you don't owe them shit? That is the craziest thing in the world to me. That is literally a dastardly, disgustingly sick way to see the world. They do owe us. There's no question about it. The question is whether they're ever going to pay us or whether or not we have the ability and the will to extract payment. I would say that it starts with awareness, number one. That's where people like me and Dr. Anderson can have conversations. I sat down with Dr. Anderson and I brought him into the Black Wealth Academy as a guest. I brought him in and I said, "Dr. Anderson, do you think that Black people deserve reparations?" He said, "Of course they deserve reparations. Let me explain why."

You know what he did? He did his thing. He's brilliant. Creating that awareness, giving people information so that they have ammunition to make these arguments when they're talking to people in the office or whatever ... Then also, you lay out reparations. I believe reparations, as a community, should be laid out as a condition for our forgiveness. If you want us to really move past the past, if you want us to go with you to the Dr. King dinner and hold hands and sing We Shall Overcome and Kumbaya, then you need to be ready to talk about reparations too, Mr. White Man. Because you're not going to get my forgiveness for nothing. Even mobsters have that rule.

If you want forgiveness from The Family you better show up with money. You better show up with some money to make up for what you did to The Family. If you show up just with an "I apologize," no, we're going to still have you whacked. You understand? Ultimately, I think that reparations should be laid out as a condition for our forgiveness. We're going to coexist with you. We're not going to kill you. We're not going to fight back necessarily. We're not going to pull up our guns and start a revolution but, at the same time, we're certainly not going to act like everything's okay because our community's destroyed and you did it.

Your ancestors did it. You own all this wealth because your ancestors stole it from us and we're not going to forget it. We're going to teach that to our kids and grandkids and this is going to be a part of every inch of the Black cultural tradition.

First thing we're going to teach our kids is how white people screwed you over. Then we're going to teach you how to overcome it. Right? I think that's perfectly fine. Here's the thing. You lay out the groundwork. You create the awareness. You set the conditions. Everybody's on the same page so maybe one day there's an opportunity. Maybe one day you get Hillary Clinton in the White House and she doesn't understand why Black people haven't forgiven her for the fact that her husband put more Black men in prison than any president in recent American history.

Well, what do we say to Hillary? We say, "We might forgive you, Hillary, but we're all thinking about reparations." "What are you going to say about reparations, Hillary?" Then you may watch her squirm in her seat and, eventually, Hillary understands power. Hillary responds to power. Hillary might come back and say, "You know what? To get more votes in the Black community, I am going to make a reparations proposal. I'll be the first president in American history to make a proposal to Congress that African Americans receive reparations." Is it going to go through? I don't know. It may take 100 years, 200 years, but I think the conversation should be had. I really do. It's a no brainer to me.

There you go. You asked a second question about how to obtain it. That's one example. We can talk about reparations all day, but I definitely agree that it's important to talk about. Michael Griffith says, "Peace." How are you doing, Michael? Good to see you. He says, "In terms of cash for emergency savings, is it best to have it in cash equivalent form, i.e. savings or money market account, or is it best to go ahead and invest savings into stocks so that it's still working?" You know what? I would say that, with cash, cash is ... Do you remember that Chris Rock movie that was really funny?

I forget. It was so funny. Chris Rock and Eddie Murphy, they make some of the funniest movies. Some of them don't do that well, though. Anyway, Chris had this movie where he died and came back to life, but he came to life as an old white guy. I don't remember what it was called. I think it was Heaven After Earth or something. I don't remember what it was called. Anyway, there was one part where Chris was talking about insurance. He was saying, "Insurance should be called 'In case shit.' You only need it in case shit happens." Cash is like your "in case shit." You want to have something that's liquid.

Liquidity of an asset is measured by how quickly it can be converted into cash in case shit happens. In case you need money to pay for something. You never want to have a portfolio that is really super illiquid. That puts you in a bad situation because there's nothing worse than to be sitting on a million-dollar asset and have no cash to even pay a $10,000 invoice. Because what can happen is that you could be forced into bankruptcy, which would require you to sell your million-dollar asset at a substantial discount because it has to be liquidated quickly.

Anything that gets liquidated quickly, meaning turned into cash quickly, is usually going to have a chop on the price to get people to pay quickly. If I live in a $2 million home and I'm behind on my taxes and I can't get the money to pay my taxes, and I have to liquidate that home quickly, you think they're going to sell that house for $2 million?

No. Maybe they'll sell it for $1.5 or something like that. In fact, a lot of people get rich by having liquidity and coming in when liquidity is rare. It's like having bottles of water when you're in the desert and people are thirsty so they'll pay anything for water, so you control the game at that point. There were people with liquidity who came in and made a killing in Detroit because they're buying whole entire city blocks.

People in Australia are buying entire city blocks in Detroit because they see that this is a struggling city with little liquidity. There are many other examples. Warren Buffett takes advantage of a lack of liquidity with major corporations. When he sees a company struggling, he can identify why the company's struggling. He tries to figure it out. He says, "Is it because they have bad management? Is it because just they had an unfortunate experience and the stock market overreacted? Is it because they need a cash injection and they can't get capital?" Or whatever. If he sees a liquidity problem, then Warren Buffett comes in with liquidity and buys this company on the cheap and makes it strong and whole again because he sees the company as a fixer-upper.

Ultimately, you want to think very carefully when you start your business or just in your life because your home is your first small business, in case you don't know that. Your life and your home are your first small business. If you manage that small business incorrectly, it's going to be hard to build another business. That's why, when I tell people when you're choosing who you marry, when you're choosing how you raise your kids, when you're choosing how to run your household, all that, you have to think about that in a business framework to make sure that it doesn't become so disruptive that it inhibits your ability to build something else.

I'll say that to these brothers out here, these young guys making baby after baby after baby and I'm like, "You've already F'd up your first small business so you're not going to be able to build nothing else. Don't even come to my Black Wealth Boot Camp. You need to go to the penis control camp or the child support camp because you're going to be broke for the rest of your life. Your ability to do much of anything now is disrupted because these choices you already made are going to just be almost like a virus in terms of your ability to do anything else." Ultimately, you want to think about that.

Liquidity is an important part of that. Always think about, "How much money do I have that's being flipped?" Dame Dash uses that term about flipping. Dame teaches a class in the Black business school with me. You should check it out. It's at IntelligentBossMoves.com. I'll give you guys the link. You want to ask yourself, "How much of my money am I flipping?" Meaning, how much money is in illiquid investments, and how much of my money can I get access to overnight? You might have a ratio like 10%. If I have $20,000 in investments, $2,000, 10% of that should be in places where I can get the money quickly. It doesn't have to be in cash, but it has to be in something that's pretty liquid.

The good thing, though, is that the stock market is relatively liquid. You buy stock in major corporations, it's going to be pretty liquid. The only problem you have to worry about is that stock prices go up and down. If you buy big, stable companies like GM and Ford and stuff like that, you'll see the range of the stock price doesn't evolve very much over time so you can always go to your Ameritrade account, hit sell, sell some stock, get that cash, and use that to pay for whatever financial emergency you have.

This leads me to a conversation about competing with other black owned businesses. In order to unpack this, let's look at two businesses as a case study and I will loop it back to black enterprises.

Uber, which I discussed previously, seemingly came out of nowhere. The concept was such a threat that the mayor of New York tried to keep them out of the city. Every city that they go to, the cab drivers don't want them there. They go to cities like Las Vegas, and the cab drivers threaten to kill the Uber drivers and break their legs. Yet, they still go there. I went to Europe. I went to England, Paris, and Spain this summer. I visited England and I took Uber. Paris, I took Uber. Spain, I took Uber. It was all on my app. Uber is amazing. They were there within five minutes.

If you are a new company like Krazy Rides, you have to do something to distinguish your brand.

You're not trying to go head to head with Uber, you're just saying, "Hey, look we do a few things Uber doesn't do." You know what? I actually like Krazy Rides. I think you could survive because I see that you guys do long distance trips, of over 45 miles. That means maybe you can market to college students. Going local, getting a ride around the city, that might be a little tough because you are head to head with Uber. But you mention taking tours of cities, I don't know that Uber does that. Getting picked up? Uber does that.

You do at least a few things that are different from Uber. I don't know if this is your company, I assume it's not your company, maybe you work with the company. Then again, it could be yours. Either way, I like it. I think you can find your lane, you just have to make sure you understand the importance of avoiding going head to head with the big boys. It's like going to war.

When the Revolutionary War took place, the Americans knew they couldn't fight head to head with the British with a traditional fighting style. They had to go guerrilla. They had to pick and choose their spots. That's what I think you want to do, is pick and choose your spots. If you pick and choose your spots, maybe you can get the scraps that Uber can't quite pick up.

I know it sounds bad, makes you feel like a scavenger, but I'm sorry. If you're in the jungle and the lion shows up to eat the dead deer and you want to eat too and you're as big as a squirrel or whatever, you don't run up and try to take the lion's food because he's going to eat you too. You understand? Maybe you wait until the lion eats and then you eat what the lion leaves behind. That could work. I know that sounds like such a wimpy way to go about doing business, but you've got to be smart enough to know, as they said in that song The Gambler, you've got to know when to hold them, know when to fold them.

This is what makes for good competition and growth, whether a company is black owned or not.

This is why I strongly encourage entrepreneurship with black folks. Corporate America is not a good place to leverage your future. These companies don't have any loyalty. To play off of a popular song, these *companies ain't loyal*. They really aren't. You dedicate your life to them and you give them everything and they just make adjustments. They don't care about the human factor.

I would look to create options for myself. We talked about things like being an Uber driver. If you've got that car in the driveway, that might be a good way to make some money. As far as the former colleagues who've turned their back on you, you've got to move on and find new colleagues. No matter what life you're living, there's always another life you could be living somewhere else. No matter who your friends are, there are always other people you can have in your circle of friends.

Never ever get to the point where you think that what you left behind is all you got. That's really important. You've got to look outward and look upward and look at the future. Don't look backward. Don't look down. Don't look at the past if the past is not giving you what you need. The more time you spend focusing on what you don't have, the less time you can spend seeing all the possibilities that may lay in front of you. A lot of people go through life like that. They spend all their time looking at the past, looking at what they lost, looking at what they don't have anymore.

Now, what aspect of your financial well-being that you can leverage is your investments, specifically ETFs and mutual funds. ETF's are exchange traded funds. What is an exchange traded fund? An exchange traded fund is something you can buy, actually, on the stock market that tracks a specific index for you. For example, there are ETF's for the S&P500. Let's say that you want to take all the guesswork out of buying stock and you just say, "I just want something that's going to track the Dow. When the Dow goes up, I want to make money. When the Dow goes down, I'll lose money. I just want to follow the Dow. I don't want to try to pick the right companies because I don't want to get into all that."

You can buy an exchange traded fund that tracks the Dow. You can buy an exchange traded fund that tracks what the index of small stocks is doing. You can buy an exchange traded fund that tracks with international stocks are doing. Mutual funds have managers that are picking the right stocks and trying to make the right guesses on what's going to do well.

ETF's don't have all that. ETF's are just like you buy it, it tracks an index, and that's it. I'm not sure exactly where it stands now, but I think that ETF's will have a lower transaction cost and things like that. Mutual funds tend to charge a fee for you to be included. How does a mutual fund work?

Basically, most people don't have the time to sit and analyze stocks all day. What they do is they setup situations where you'll have a group of fund managers who are experts, who went to school for this. They'll collect money from a lot of people. It's a little bit like crowdfunding. They'll collect a thousand dollars from this person, a million from that person, a hundred thousand from that person, and they pile it up and they create this billion-dollar fund. They'll spend the whole day figuring out where to put pieces of this billion-dollar fund. They claim that by pulling everything together, everybody's able to make a little more money than they would if they were trying to do it on their own. Some theories support that idea. That's how a mutual fund works versus an ETF.

People will often ask me about investing in Africa. You know what? I'm not really sure what the status is on stock markets in Africa. I know that there are ways to buy stock in Africa. I remember working with a guy at University of Maryland 12, 13 years ago who wanted help with developing stock markets in Africa.

I know the markets are not as great as they are in other countries, but there are ways to do that. What you have to be really careful about is making sure whatever market you pick, that you're picking what they call a liquid, well-functioning market. That's a market where everything's going to be on the up and up. I don't know if you guys will remember this, but one thing we talked about is that the way a stock gets valued is all based on information. A big function of that information is based on transparency and consistency, which is a risk measure.

Think about it like this. How comfortable would you be if you were giving me your money, and I was running a company, and I told you nothing? I filed no reports. I didn't tell you what I was doing with that money. I could be spending it on my mistress. I went behind this curtain and just took your money and did whatever I wanted with it. You would probably not feel so safe doing that, right? What if I said, "I'm going to invest your money and I'm going to show you everything. I'm going to give you complete transparency. You can come in. You can see what we're doing. You can read the reports. I'll answer your questions, all of that stuff." That will make you feel more comfortable, right?

The price of a company stock is largely dependent upon that form of transparency and that form of consistency. When a stock has transparency and consistency, it's typically going to have a higher value than a company that has no transparency, no consistency, and a lot of risk. That actually extrapolates into an entire market. If you look at world stock markets around the world, markets that have a lot of transparency, consistency, and low risk tend to have higher values than markets that have very little transparency, a lot of volatility, and also a lot of risk.

It can even be political risk. There are some countries where you can invest your money and the government could decide, "We're just going to take over this company. We're just going to own it. It's ours. We're taking it." This has happened to investors. This has happened to people on many occasions. Countries where that kind of thing tends to happen, where there's a lot of political risk, they don't get a lot of investors.

A lot of people aren't in a rush to give money to places where the government might step in and just take everything. The New York Stock Exchange tends to do pretty well because there's a lot of that transparency, a lot of that consistency. There's very low political risk. President Obama's not going to create a law tomorrow saying, "We're taking over every corporation in America." People feel comfortable putting their money here. When there's more money flowing in, it increases the prices of the assets. Do you understand?

When you're investing in a third world country, Africa or

anywhere else, look for these factors. Make sure you do your research to make sure that you don't send over a bunch of money and then have somebody tell you, "Sorry, we lost your money." You're like, "What happened? Can I see a report?" "No, we don't issue reports." Or, "Here's a report. We're going to give you this report. It's full of fake information because we have no regulatory body here that's going to make sure this information's accurate." That's why the securities and exchange commission exists is to increase confidence in the stock market. They are very, very focused on making sure that confidence is always strong because when confidence starts to drop, prices start to plummet.

It could literally lead to a trillion dollar drop in economic value in the American stock exchange by doing something that creates a lack of confidence in the market. A terrorist attack reduces confidence. A run on banks reduces confidence. Crazy information, if somebody releases misinformation, they say, "Mark Zuckerberg says that Facebook is a fraud and that no one should sign up for his company." Guess what? Facebook's value's going to drop from $300 billion to about $250 billion in a matter of seconds. Those factors really play an important role. Make sure you look for that when you invest overseas.

Christian asks, nope, we already answered that question, Christian. Sorry. Michelle mentions that she says, "I had a friend who was a drug dealer that got killed. His whole family went down including the mom, and got 20 years for keeping the drug books." That relates to what we were talking about earlier about how the Feds can be when it comes to that money. It's scary. It's really scary.

But, what's scarier than that is the amount of interest Black folks are paying for student loans—pay them off if you can. Student loan debt is a severe epidemic. It's one of the great challenges that we're faced with right now as a country. Student loan debt is what they call a bubble. It's one of the bubbles in the American economy. A bubble is something that could easily burst. That means that if that market for student loan debt suddenly becomes unstable, it could really cause a ripple effect through the entire economy. It hasn't burst yet but what's happening is the default rates are slowly going up.

A large percentage of former college students are just not paying the loans back because they're like, "We don't have the jobs that pay enough money to pay back this much debt." A lot of jobs, the good jobs, a lot of them have been shipped overseas. But American consumers are used as a source of cash for corporations that will make a product like the Air Jordans or whatever in other countries for $10, $16, but sell them in the United States because Americans have an addiction to consumption, and Americans have an extreme willingness to take on extra debt to maintain a particular lifestyle.

What happens is you ultimately do become a slave to that debt. The only thing that I'm afraid of now is that one day we'll get to a point where the corporations that own our government will go to our politicians and force them to write laws that say, "If you don't pay your debt we're going to put you in jail." At that point, we truly will be slaves to debt. We truly will be slaves. "Either pay the debt or go to jail." They'll treat it just like child support. Don't think that it can't happen.

You've got to be really careful about debt, especially student loan debt when you send your kids to college. I'm a big fan of either state schools, which tend to be far cheaper than private schools, or if you send them to good entrepreneurship programs like the ones that we have here in the Black business school, I've seen a lot of people start off and do really well doing that kind of stuff. I just did a business deal with a young guy. I always say that he was 23 and I found out he's actually 29. But he didn't go to college. I'm going to pay him a lot of money to help me with something because he has a skill.

If you have a skill then that nullifies a lot of the whole need to have a degree. A degree is only a proxy to say that you have skill. I can't really prove to you I have skill. If I know how to build a house, I can show you a house that I've built. If I'm a manager, let's say I want to come to your company. I want to do management. That's pretty vague. What do I have to show you that I have the skill? I have a piece of paper. When you talk about entrepreneurship, entrepreneurship exposes you. If you're a person that's got paper and no skill then go try to run a business. Your customers will tell you if you have skill or not.

When you have no sales that will show that you have no skill. Ultimately, I think there are a lot of ways to be successful. In fact, I encourage my kids. When I talk to my own kids, I tell them, "Don't even pick a career. Don't even tell anybody what you do for a living. You can tell them what you actually *do,* but don't define yourself. Don't say, 'I'm an accountant.' 'I'm a teacher.' 'I'm this.' 'I'm that.' You don't have to do that anymore. You could just say, 'I run a website.'" My daughter does hair. She blogs. She has a show on social media. She does a lot of different things. She's not in a box anymore.

She's very, very happy not being in the box. Don't feel like you've got to get in the box. Don't put your kids in a box. You don't have to do that. Make entrepreneurship a part of your family's culture. That's important. In fact, whether it's understanding cashflow, or saving for retirement, building a business, taxes, or credit repair and budgeting make this a part of our dinner table conversations and discussions during car rides to and from school and other activities.

As I am bringing the book to a close, I want to encourage everyone who is reading this to check out The Black Wealth Academy; it meets just like the boot camp. We meet twice a week and we have office hours. We even have a private Facebook group. We also have hundreds of hours of content that you can read and view to continue your own learning and quest for financial efficacy.

The cool thing about the academy is that because it's longer we're able to do more stuff. We're able to go deeper in to theories. If people ask me for a specialized lecture on a certain topic, I can do that. Also, we have really thoughtful and knowledgeable guests. We've had Tariq Nasheed who created the *Hidden Colors* documentary series. We brought in Dr.

Claude Anderson. We brought in leadership expert Nicole Price. We intentionally bring in a lot of different people who can add value to your ability to build something of your own.

That's what I respect. I respect Black people who build things. I don't really necessarily care if a white man gave you a great job. I mean, I'm happy for you, I think that's good but, honestly, deep down I'm thinking, "Gosh, that's pretty limited thinking, a little bit." It's not to be critical, but it's saying I'm not really impressed with the person who gets the job as much as I'm impressed with the person who created the job that they just gave you. That's the real boss. That's the man of your house.

You might not be the man of your house. You've got to really look at that in an honest way. It's no disrespect to those of you who've got promotions this week. I'm happy for you. But build something of your own. That's what I think will matter to your children in the long term.

And if you aren't quite ready to take on that role, find a business mentor who will guide you through the process. When you pick people as your mentors, first thing is you don't always have to tell people that they're your mentor. You just watch them and observe what they do. Also, you want to think about mentorship not so much as a charitable event. You don't walk up to somebody that's really busy, that has a lot of stuff that they're trying to do and say, "Will you mentor me?" because they will probably tell you that, "I can't."

You also don't walk up to someone and say, "I don't have anything. I can't offer anything. I'm not doing anything that's really working, but can you mentor me? Because I really need your help."

People might give you a little bit of charity but charity is not sustainable. They're not going to always be able to give you the amount of time that you're really going to need. They're not going to be able to spend the time with you that's really going to make you good at what you want to do. I go through that because every day, 10 people ask me to mentor them, every single day. I thought about this, and I was thinking, "What's the best way that people actually learn from me?" The people that learn from me are the people that work with me, the people that bring something to the table, that say, "I can dedicate 30 hours a week." If they want to get paid, they don't ask for a lot of money, if they have a skill or something like that.

I can't have that many people on my team, but the people who are on my team are really grinding with me every day; they have access to me because we're always trying to solve a problem together. We're always working on something. They get to see exactly how we do things, right? I would say that if you approach anybody as a potential mentor, come bearing gifts. Come there and say, "Here's what I'm going to do for you. Here's what I can do to help you. Here's what you can do to help me." Then it becomes a trade. It becomes easier for it to work.

I learned that in my Ph.D. program because I thought that professors should want to work with us because we were the students and because that was their job. I quickly learned that if you weren't offering anything to those guys, they weren't going to work with you. They were just going to blow you off. Or they were going to give you a few minutes but then they had work to do. Just understand that everybody's got work to do. Keep that in mind.

That's why I'm not that big on climbing a ladder to get to the top of somebody else's house. That's a little bit strange. Let's see here. We'll do a couple more questions then we'll take off. Howard Tibbs asks about Amazon delivery jobs. I think that Amazon delivery jobs are a good way to make extra money, too. I shared that link on the boot camp page. Amazon's now doing delivery.

Amazon's making big moves. If you want to understand how a small company grows into something special, go look at Amazon, read their history and just read how they grew. They're also an interesting, compelling lesson about the valuations of stock markets and how they occur. Amazon had many years where they weren't making a penny but they were worth billions. People were like, "Why is this company worth over a billion dollars when they haven't made any money?" Because people were looking at future revenue generating possibilities. That's one interesting thing about Amazon. They saw the future and they saw what this company would be worth.

The other interesting thing about Amazon is that most of the money that they make doesn't even go to them. Most of the money they make, they have to give it to their affiliates, to people that sell products on their platform. That goes back to what I was telling you guys about partnerships, affiliate programs, and how that can be a great way to boost your business. That's why I tell you, "If you have a great company and it fits my audience, I want to be an affiliate for your product." When I have a great product like the Black Wealth Boot Camp and the Black business school, we have an affiliate program. You can be an affiliate and tell your friends about them. They sign up then you get a percentage.

It might be your first step to getting off the plantation. That's the other interesting thing about Amazon. Another interesting thing about Amazon as they are growing and literally conquering the freaking world, is that Amazon is now at a point where they are about to literally eliminate their need for UPS, FedEx, or the United States Postal Service. There are people that are low-key speculating that Amazon is trying to create its own fleet of trucks and planes so that they can do their own delivery with their own stuff. They're going to have trucks, planes, cars, drones and regular drivers that are similar to an Uber kind of thing. Amazon is killing the game right now.

In fact, there was some big news. I had some stock options in Amazon. Suddenly, I went to my portfolio and I saw it made a couple thousand dollars that day. Of course, I was smiling. I was like, "What's going on? My Amazon options just shot through the roof." Then I looked up the news. Whenever you see your stock price move up or down, there's always news.

Stock markets move based on news and information. What was the news of Amazon? I looked it up. The news was that Amazon's data services company, where they do this cloud data storage for companies, this little side business that everybody thought wasn't a big deal, turns out that this cloud storage, their side hustle, was worth $160 billion. Everybody's like, "Holy crap."

They're controlling this game over here, too. Amazon, to me, is fascinating to me because they're just a company that just has this extraordinary vision. I don't know if this is all coming from the CEO Bezos, but that is an awesome company. In fact, you know they bought the Washington Post. Bezos, he bought the Washington Post. This is what's funny. This is how liquidity can allow a mobile thinker to take advantage of a dinosaur. The Washington Post used to be worth about $2.5 billion in the late 90s before the internet really got into heavy use as a source of media. $2.5 billion. Do you know that Bezos was able to buy that company a few years later for $250 million?

This was literally about a tenth of what the company was worth because you had dinosaurs that didn't understand. You had this family that was making all this money from this newspaper, that didn't understand the importance of adjusting to the times. They didn't adjust to the times and they got hammered. The internet has led to a massive wealth transfer from backward thinking people to forward thinking people. That's why you want to be on the forefront of technology, education and understanding what's happening in the world so you can be one of the people that's taking advantage of the fact that there are people who are stuck in their ways and aren't willing to adjust.

It's happening in the Black community, too. *Ebony Magazine* is going through that a little bit. Ebony's hanging on. I love *Ebony*. I've written in *Ebony* many times. I don't have nothing negative to say about *Ebony* or the management, per se, but I'm telling you. They've missed out on some major opportunities because they were so used to making money the old way that they didn't think about how to make money the new way. Some of these other companies like *Essence* are gone. *Essence* isn't ours anymore. That belongs to white folks. BET belongs to white folks.

Ultimately, the inability to adapt gives you the keys and the tickets to your own economic extermination. How much you learn is important. How much education you have matters. But what matters more is your ability to consistently be educated in a dynamic fashion and to consistently be able to adapt. That's it.

Because I really think that we're in the middle of this amazing cultural revolution in our community, and I'm telling you, in 50 years, or maybe a little more than 50 years you're going to see a whole different Black community. You're going to see literally millions of Black people that are focused on wealth building and ownership, and all the things that I'm saying that just sound so radical and revolutionary now, it's going to be old hat. It's going to be standard education for most Black kids in America.

That's the vision I have. I know that that's the vision we're going to achieve. But I need your help in making that happen. I love all of you guys. I hope that you learned something new about being a millionaire and that something that you read in this book will propel you to build more, soar higher, and position your children to be great.

None of us get to this moment alone. We had people who helped mold us, inspire us and mentor us. I hope that in some capacity, my words have done that for you. As with any book that contains a wealth of information, I encourage you to go back through this, share it with your family and use the information that is embedded within here to think and act like a millionaire.

ABOUT THE AUTHOR

Dr. Boyce D. Watkins is one of the leading financial scholars and social commentators in America. He advocates for education, economic empowerment and social justice and has changed the definition of what it means to be a Black scholar and leader in America.

He is one of the founding fathers of the field of Financial Activism – The objective of creating social change through the use of conscientious capitalism. He is a Blue Ribbon Speaker with Great Black Speakers, Inc. and one of the most highly sought after public figures in the country.

In addition to publishing a multitude of scholarly articles on finance, education and black social commentary, Dr. Watkins has presented his message to millions, making regular appearances in various national media outlets, including CNN, Good Morning America, MSNBC, FOX News, BET, NPR, Essence Magazine, USA Today, The Today Show, ESPN, The Tom Joyner Morning Show and CBS Sports.

Educationally, Dr. Watkins earned BA and BS degrees with a triple major in Finance, Economics and Business Management. In college, he was selected by the Wall Street Journal as the Outstanding Graduating Senior in Finance. He then earned a Master's Degree in Mathematical Statistics from University of Kentucky and a PhD in Finance from Ohio State University and was the only African-American in the world to earn a PHD in Finance during the year 2002. He is the founder of The Black Wealth Bootcamp, The Black Business School and The Your Black World coalition, which have a collective total of 300,000 subscribers and 1.4 million social media followers world-wide.

In 2017, Simmons College, an HBCU in Kentucky, announced the creation of The Dr. Boyce Watkins Economic Empowerment Institute, where the goal is to develop black economic leaders for the 21st century and beyond.

**Dr. Watkins is also the founder of The Black Business School and The Black Wealth Bootcamp, which have over 35,000 students.**